# GIVE MY FRIEND A PASS

Author:  Fhito Polycarpe

Alex and Frantz have been friends since elementary school. They grew up on the same street. They graduated High School the same year and attended the same college after high school graduation. After obtaining their bachelor degrees..Alex starts a new job at a private financial firm..Frantz works for an accounting firm not too far from where his friend Alex works..The owner of the firm where Alex works is a very powerful and notorious businessman by the name of Jim Castillo..His young and beautiful wife Katy works for the firm..She is Alex boss..It did not take long for her to display special attention to Alex..Alex and Frantz are having lunch..Let's sit at a table nearby and listen:

Alex: What's going on?

Frantz: I am very hungry..I went to the gym this morning and I did not eat much

Alex: I saw you drinking your shake

Frantz: That was just that..I did not eat anything else

Alex: Order you some food my brother

Frantz: Of course..Why you look so happy..Why you have this smile in your face

Alex: I love my job

Frantz: Good for you..My boss is not a bad guy..But..I think he gets overwhelmed too easily..And when that happened he transferred the pressure down to us..When we are approaching the end of the year..It's even worse

Alex: Why is that?

Frantz: Book reconciliations

Alex: I see..Those were my worst accounting classes

Frantz: Where do you get this little bracelet you are wearing?

Alex: Oh this?

Frantz: Yes..That?

Alex: My boss put it in my arm this morning

Frantz: Your boss?..She is married..Right?

Alex: I know..What this has to do with her being married?

Frantz: Don't be naïve..You think she just put a bracelet on your arm for no reason?

Alex: I don't even see it this way

Frantz: People don't just put a bracelet in anybody's arm..It looks expensive too

Alex: It might be..She told me that all these little stones are real diamonds

Frantz: You sure know who her husband is?..Right?

Alex: Jim..Big Jim

Frantz: Exactly..Jim Castillo..You heard the story about that pool guy who disappeared

Alex: I heard of it..I am not a pool guy

Frantz: C'mon silly..Don't be a fool..The guy was the pool maintenance guy..One day Jim came back home and saw her talking to the guy..He he has not been seen since

Alex: Those are often rumors my dude

Frantz: He was being investigated by the police for it..It's the true

Alex: What are you trying to make me do..You are telling me scary stories..And I am wearing a bracelet that his wife gave me..You are trying to make me cut my arm off

Frantz: Very funny Alex..If Jim found out..You might lose your arm..At least

Alex: Listen brother..I am no punk..Since when you became a punk?..You pledged in college..You went through it all..Now you are making some money..And you became soft

Frantz: This is not being soft..This is the man wife Alex

Alex: Oh my god..Listen to you Frantz..What is the crime I have committed brother

Frantz: Not a crime..But

Waitress: Are you guys ready to order

Alex: Hi Caroline..How are you..You look beautiful today..Bring me the usual

Waitress: Ok..Just the steak..No sauce..Right?

Alex: No sauce

Frantz: Same thing for me..With a lot of sauce..I am the opposite of this guy

Waitress: I see that..This is why you guys get along so well

Alex: I would not say get along so well..This guy is a pain on my neck..Always trying to preach me..What do you think of my bracelet Caroline?

Waitress: I think it's nice..It's look like a lady bracelet..I think both men and women can wear it..Those diamonds are real?

Alex: I don't wear anything fake

Waitress: Why you don't like his bracelet?

Frantz: Well..It's just not for me

Alex: You damn right it's not for you bro..It's for me

Frantz: Very funny

Waitress: What you guys want to drink?

Alex: A coke for me..And of course seltzer water for my old man here..By the way I saw you at the club the other night Caroline..This uniform does not do you justice..You were looking fantastic in that dress..It was begging for mercy

Waitress: You are too funny..You should have stopped by and say hello

Alex: No..I was good..You were in a group of twenty guys

Waitress: It was my friend Brittney's birthday..Not twenty guys..You are exaggerating..You guys want to eat or not?

Frantz: I am starving..If he asked you one more question..I am punching him dead in his mouth

Alex: Go..Go Caroline..My god..You see the hatred..You are so violent Frantz

Frantz: Violent? You will know violence if you keep messing with Jim Castillo's wife

Alex: C'mon Frantz..You are being too dramatic about this whole thing..She is my boss..What am I supposed to do?..I am supposed to do what my boss wants me to do

Frantz: That is within the realm of your work

Alex: Wearing the bracelet is not within the realm of work..That's what you are trying to say

Frantz: Your phone is ringing

Alex: Be quiet that's her calling me

Frantz: Are you crazy?

Alex: Shut up Frantz..Hello

Katy: Hello..It's me Katy..Where are you?

Alex: I am at lunch

Katy: Excuse me..You had a date..This is why you left your computer on

Alex: Not a date..I am with my buddy here

Katy: Even if you were on a date..You would not have told me

Alex: I would have told you..Why not?

Katy: I would have been so hurt

Alex: What do you mean?

Katy: I will explain later..By the way..Do you like the bracelet?

Alex: I think it's nice..But..It's your bracelet..You didn't give it to me

Katy: I want you to keep it..So you can always remember that I am your boss

Alex: Really?

Katy: Yes..Even when you are at home

Alex: Ok..I would not ask why..By the way you want me to bring you something to eat?

Katy: Aren't you coming back to the office?

Alex: Yes..Sure

Katy: Well then..Anyway..I will see you later..You miss me?..Don't you?

Alex: I did not hear you?

Katy: Do you miss me?

Alex: Uh..Yeah..Of course I miss you

Katy: See you soon

Alex: See you soon

Frantz: That was Jim's wife on the phone..Right?

Alex: Yeah

Frantz: You are a dead man walking..You are so dead

Alex: C'mon dude..What did I do?..I was not the one

Frantz: Alex..Every time you get yourself in trouble..I am the one you come to..To save you..I am not going to be involved in this one..I can see it coming toward you full speed

Alex: What is coming toward me?

Frantz: A tornado called Jim..And you are right on the path of it

Alex: Frantz..What do I do..Be rude to her..I am not married

Frantz: Well..She is..It only takes one of the two to be married to make it wrong..Not both..If she were not married..Fine..No problem at all..If your boss is not married and she has feeling for you..It's completely fine..People fall in love every day..Love is blind..But..She is married..Not only is she married..She is married to Jim Castillo

Alex: I am tired of you telling me about that Jim..What are you a scarecrow for Jim?

Frantz: I am not a scarecrow for Jim..Nor that I will be your protector

Alex: You are just too dramatic my brother..I haven't touched the woman..You are talking as she ran away with me

Frantz: Exactly..Running away is what I would consider if I were you..I heard your conversation with her..This is not going be good for you

Alex: You are listening to people's conversation Frantz..That's not good for you either

Waitress: You guys are still arguing?

Alex: He is just annoying

Waitress: Ok guys..I have your steaks the way you wanted them

Alex: Looking and smelling good too..Look at his eyes..Fire is coming out of them..Take your time brother

Frantz: I am starving..I told you I haven't eaten anything since morning

Alex: Now..I understand why you are so cranky

Frantz: I am not cranky at all

Waitress: Ok guys..If you need anything let me know

Alex: Sure..Thanks..You are working until what time today?

Waitress: Until two..I have classes later today

Frantz: what is she studying?

Alex:  She wants to be an actress

Frantz:  Ok..Good for her

Alex:  All jokes aside bro..I do understand the danger that exists in having a relationship with a married woman..But it is not at this point yet

Frantz:  You want her to move in with you for it to be the so called point

Alex:  I haven't made any move towards her

Frantz:  You accept a bracelet from her..You told her.. I miss you too..If those are not moves..I don't know what is

Alex:  Once she moves in to get closer or makes it a more serious thing..I will certainly stop it

Frantz:  Alright brother..Time for me to get back to work

Alex:  Me too

Frantz:  You too?

Alex:  Yeah

Frantz:  You mean to your date..Right?

Alex:  C'mon Frantz..You are always exaggerating..That was very funny though

Frantz:  Funny..But true

Alex:  Alright brother..I will see you later..You will be at the gym?

Frantz:  Not today..I worked out this morning

Alex:  When I leave the gym..I will pass by

Frantz:  Today is my date night with Nancy..Don't need your bad influence around us

Alex:  C'mon brother..That's the way you are treating your brother?..Where is the love?..You are talking as if I murder someone or something

Frantz:  There might be a murder in your future if you keep messing with Jim Castillo's wife

Alex:  Very funny..You are my favorite comedian..You know that?

Frantz:  I can be anything..One thing I am not going to be this time..Is your rescuer..I warned you in advance..From the time we were in high school..You always get yourself in some troubles..Always had to fight..Most fights I was involved in was for you

Alex: That's what brothers are for..Its' not that I could not fight..I am a black belt too Frantz..Not just you

Frantz: You made me put mine to good use

Alex: This is what I don't understand..Why a black belt is afraid of a guy called Jim..Do you know how many guys called Jim I trashed in my life?

Frantz: This one could be your last try..I have to go brother..My situation at work is a bit different from yours

Alex: How different Frantz?..You are doing volunteer work?

Frantz: Not volunteer work..It's not a date

Alex: You are just jealous brother..Are you hating?..Say it

Frantz: You are crazy..I would not like to be you..Later..Got to go

Alex: Peace brother

Frantz: Later brother


_A few minutes later..At Alex's office


Katy: Finally..You are here..It took you an eternity

Alex: Not really..Just an hour

Katy: Do you know what an hour away from you means?

Alex: What?

Katy: Nothing

Alex: What happened to my desk and my stuffs?

Katy: I have you moved in with me..From now on..You are going to be with me..In my office..My office is way too big for me alone

Alex: But..The other guys may think..You are playing favoritism

Katy: No..Not at all..I am the boss..What I want..Will be done..Do you have any questions?

Alex: No..Not really..Your husband comes to the office sometimes..How do you think he will see this?

Katy: Jim?..I don't think he will make a big deal out of it

Alex: I heard different

Katy: What did you hear?

Alex: The pool guy story

Katy: C'mon..The pool guy?..Jim came back home and found him in the patio talking with me..It's a different story

Alex: Is it true..That he disappeared?

Katy: Don't be ridiculous..What do you think of my husband Alex..A murderer..C'mon..He does have connections..But he did not do anything to that guy..Alejandro was from Mexico..I believe that he moved back to his country..Are you afraid?

Alex: I am not afraid..I don't have a country to move back to

Katy: Very funny..This is why I like you..You make me smile..Always

Alex: How do you explain me moving in your office to Jim?

Katy: If it will make you feel better..I will tell Jim..That we work closely together..Calling you on the phone is aggravating..And he will say..Ok my love..You feel better?..Less scared?

Alex: It's not for me..It's for you

Katy: All men say the same thing..It's not for me..It's for you..When in fact..They are very afraid

Alex: I am not that type Katy..I am trying to protect you..You are married..And he is your boss

Katy: My husband is not my boss..Frankly..I don't have a boss..This is why I am in charge of this office..He barely comes here..I don't know why you are making such a big deal out of it..It's not like you are sitting in my lap here..You r desk is so many feet away from mine..I want you in here because I am tired of calling you on the phone every minute..We work together

Alex: Your husband has a reputation

Katy: What reputation Alex?

Alex: Well

Katy: Well what?..If you are too afraid to work in here with me..I don't think I want you to work for me at all

Alex: You missed the point Katy..This is not about me..I am not afraid of any men..I just don't want to be the one who destroyed your marriage

Katy: You are thinking of the worst..Life is more fun than you think

Alex: Well..Let's the fun begin

Katy: Talking about fun..I have some work I want you to do for me..I want you to work on that general ledger for me today

Alex: You mean tomorrow..It's almost time to leave work..Tomorrow I will be glad to work on it

Katy: I would appreciate it if you could start working on it today..We are closing the books next week..I need it to be done..Can you at least work an hour over time?

Alex: I don't get paid over time Katy..You know that..I am on a fix salary..You want me to do volunteer work

Katy: You will be compensated for it..Trust me

Alex: I will call my workout buddies and tell them that I will be at the gym late

Katy: Please do..I really appreciate it


_An hour and a half later


Alex: It is so quiet here..I went to get some water..This place is like a ghost town

Katy: This is the way I like it..A ghost town and we are the only two survivors

Alex: Until your husband Jim finds out that I am sharing your office with you

Katy: What do you know..You don't know Jim the way I know him..Why you still have your tie on..This is not working hours..At least loose it up..Just like that..Don't you feel better?

Alex: I won't be able to work on the ledger in that pace

Katy: I will leave you alone..Let me make sure all the doors are locked

Alex: What are you worrying about..I am here

Katy: I can't trust you to protect me..You are too afraid of my husband

Alex: Very funny Katy..Don't get me wrong..If you were not married..I would fall in love with you..You showed me love..And I am dying to return the love..But you are married to the notorious Jim Castillo

Katy: You are not dying hard enough..I want you to die harder to show me your love

Alex: Where is he from..Castillo..Is he of Hispanic descent?

Katy: No..He is Italian..His parents don't even speak English..They only speak Italian

Alex: Italian..Uh?..I just don't want to be found frozen in the back of a food truck

Katy: You watched too many movies Alex..His dad may be connected..I don't think Jim is

Alex: I am not trying to find out..Why are you looking over my shoulder?

Katy: I make you nervous..I want to see your work..I am your boss..You forgot..You are so jumpy..Your neck is so warm..It burns my lips

Alex: Katy..I don't think it's safe to do that..Someone could just walk right in the hallway..The blinds are opened

Katy: No one is here..I locked all the doors..What's wrong with your belt buckle?

Alex: Katy..Your lips are so warm


_A couple hours later


Nancy: Who is calling you so many times?

Frantz: This is Alex..I will call him later..He knows tonight is my date night with you..He is just being annoying as usual

Nancy: I think you should answer the phone babe..He's been calling you non stop

Frantz: He called me fifteen times in the row

Nancy: That's not right babe..Answer the phone..He could be in a situation and needs your help

Frantz: I know Alex..He is just going to ask me..Where am I..And tell me some silly stories as usual..If you insist..I will answer it next time

Nancy: That's him again?

Frantz: Who else..Hello..Are you on fire?..If you are call the fire department..You are killing my phone Alex..You know it's my date night with Nancy

Alex: Sorry..Sorry buddy..Say hello to her for me..Listen

Frantz: What?..I am listening

Alex: I did it..I did it

Frantz: I don't understand..You did what?

Alex: I did it..C'mon man..She asked me to work late and I did it

Frantz: What you want me to say congratulations

Alex: C'mon Frantz..Don't be a hater

Frantz: I am not..It's just the circumstances are not good for that kind of stuff

Alex: I know she is married..So what?..I will be careful..When I see you I will tell you how it all happens

Frantz: You should not be concerned about that..If I were you..I would start planning my funeral

Alex: C'mon brother..You dramatize the whole thing

Frantz: Me..You are diving deeper into the drama pool every day..Don't blame me

Alex: It was so good..She got knowledge

Frantz: Stop talking..I can't talk to you now..I am on a date with Nancy

Alex: I will see you tomorrow at lunch time

Frantz: No problem

Nancy: What is he talking about?

Frantz: Nothing serious babe

Nancy: It sounds serious to me..You were very serious when you were on the phone..You were almost mad at him..What did he do?

Frantz: Nothing at all..More wine babe?

Nancy: You are changing the subject Frantz..I just don't like when you do that

Frantz: I told you babe..It is nothing that matters

Nancy: Now you are lying to me..You told him..He should prepare his funeral..What can be more serious that that

Frantz: Babe..Let's change the subject

Nancy: You have secret for me now?

Frantz: It's not your business babe..It's not even my business what he is doing..I can't tell you his personal stuffs

Nancy:  This is so strange Frantz..I told you everything about my friends

Frantz:  You don't have to..It's your choice..I just can't do that

Nancy:  If you can't tell me..We might as well end our date

Frantz:  Well..If all you want to hear is other people's business..We might as well end it..See you tomorrow

Nancy:  Are you putting me out of your apartment?

Frantz:  I am not Nancy..You said we should end the date..Did you not?

Nancy:  You are more concerned about keeping secret for your friend than our date..Right?

Frantz:  I am sorry if you took it the wrong way..But..I have a duty to protect my friend privacy..There is no reason to put his business in the streets

Nancy:  I am the streets now?

Frantz:  Try to understand me..This is not my place to tell you what he just talked to me about

Nancy:  Did he murder somebody?

Frantz:  Very funny Nancy..It would not be my place to tell you if he did

Nancy:  I feel like I don't know you right now

Frantz:  Nancy..You feel the way you want..You will get over it..You are over reacting to something that has nothing to do with you..Bye lady

Nancy:  Say you are putting me out and you will never see me at your door again

Frantz:  Stay Nancy..I have a bed here..Go lay down..Spend the night..But I won't talk to you about my friend's business..This is just not my place..Since when Nancy?..A guy told another guy a trivial story and you have so much interest in knowing what it is..What is a matter with you?

Nancy:  It is important..I heard you say prepare your funeral

Frantz:  I think you should go home and prepare your own funeral..Because if you keep acting like that you will soon have a heart attack

Nancy:  You are being so cruel..First you put me out and now you tell me to go prepare my funeral

Frantz:  Nancy..Frankly..I am tired of this futile argument..Go home..Stay..Do whatever you want..I am going to bed..I have to work tomorrow

Nancy:  I think I will stay here tonight..You are probably up to something..You are so eager for me to leave

Frantz: Nancy..Feel free..This is not the first time you stay at my place..The only thing you are not going to do..It's spending the night here and running your mouth all night..I have to sleep..Do we agree on that?

Nancy: I can talk if I want to

Frantz: I know you can..But this is my apartment..I have the right to have peace and quiet and get some sleep

Nancy: Don't worry..I will let you sleep

Frantz: Aren't you working tomorrow?

Nancy: Yes I am..Why you asked

Frantz: You were not prepared to spend the night..You didn't bring work clothes

Nancy: I stayed with you many times and I woke up early and went home..It's not that I live at the end of town..I live five minutes from you..You remember..You know what..You are acting shady Frantz..I am leaving..Good bye

Frantz: Good bye Nancy..Lock the door please

Nancy: You come and lock the door

Frantz: You are being mean now

Nancy: I am the mean one

Frantz: I love you

Nancy: Whatever


_The next day..Alex meets Frantz for Lunch


Alex: Hey buddy..What's going on..You did not answer me

Frantz: I did not hear you..What did you say?

Alex: I said what's up..And you just ignored me

Frantz: Sorry..I did not hear you

Alex: C'mon brother..We are the only two people here..Who you thought I was talking to

Frantz: I am trying not to get too involve in your conversations..Now..Nancy is not talking to me..I called her this morning and she did not answer the phone

Alex: Why is that..Not because of me..Don't blame me brother..That's why you want to kill me?

Frantz: I am not trying to kill you..You are already trying to kill yourself

Alex: How so..Because I had sex with a lady I work with..This is a free country..This is America..People have the right to choose who they want to be with

Frantz: Right..That is if she were single..If she were divorced..But..She is happily married..Where do you think your relationship with her is heading..What is the future holds for you and her

Alex: First of all..I wouldn't say she is happily married

Frantz: How do you know that?

Alex: Bro..I was there yesterday..I saw how passionate she was making love to me

Frantz: That's does not translate she is not happily married..She probably wants to satisfy a fantasy

Alex: That was no fantasy brother..You want to hear something

Frantz: What?

Alex: She told me that she loves me..What do you say to that?

Frantz: Let me ask you this..You think she will leave her husband for you?

Alex: I can't predict the future..But..Nothing is impossible

Frantz: I can't predict the future either..But..I can't see some serious problems in your future

Alex: Relax Frantz..You are too uptight

Frantz: Uptight..That's the way you call it..Now..My girl is not talking to me because of you..I started to feel the wind from the storm to come

Alex: There will be no storm brother

Frantz: Dude..Seriously..This is what I suggest..You hit it..Quit it before t's too late..I am talking to you as your brother..If she was not married..It would have been wonderful..This is too dangerous brother

Alex: I hear you..I will think about it


_The next day at the office

Katy: Are you working on the ledger Alex?

Alex: Yes I am

Katy: You did not do much on it last night

Alex: You gave me no chance

Katy: Don't blame it on me

Jim: Good morning..Good morning

Katy: Jim..What are you doing here?..I thought you were playing golf today?

Jim: I left some golf clubs in here I just came to retrieve them

Katy: Jim..This is Alex..I told you about Alex

Jim: You sure did

Katy: Hey Tony..Can't you say hello?

Tony: It's morning..I am not a morning person

Jim: Believe him..All the people that he killed..They were killed in the morning..He is just not a morning person

Katy: Very funny Jim..Alex..Come say hello to Jim and Tony

Jim: His desk is actually in your office?

Katy: Yes..I told you Jim..I did not like the calling on the phone all the time

Tony: So..Alex..That's your name..Right?

Alex: Yes..Alex

Tony: Jim..Alex moved in with your wife..What should you do with him?

Jim: I don't know

Alex: It was her idea..Not moved in..It's just my desk

Jim: And your chair too..Right?

Tony: The kid is shaking already

Katy: Guys..Don't come here to bother my employee..Alex is a very nice guy..The best worker..He has never been late

Tony: So..Katy is your boss..Right?

Alex: Yes she is

Tony: You work under her

Alex: Well..I don't work under her..She is just my boss

Tony: He is shaking really bad

Alex: Very funny..I am not shaking sir

Jim: Are you sure..You are going to behave yourself while inside my wife's office?

Alex: Sure..It's just work..Nothing but work

Katy: Guys..I want you out of my office..Alex has work to do..Get out Tony..And you too Jim..You have your golf clubs?

Jim: Yes I do..Goodbye honey..See you later..Nice to meet you young man..Don't be so afraid

Alex: I am fine..I am not afraid at all

Katy: Bye honey..See you later


_Jim and Tony left the office..Alex's heart was beating out of his chest


Katy: Look at you..You look so guilty..You were sweating so much

Alex: You are so right..I look so nervous..I don't think we should do this..It's too scary..They look like assassins

Katy: My husband?..No..He is the nicest guy

Alex: Tony looks scary

Katy: Tony looks a little bit intimidating..Because of his size..You should not worry about anything

Alex: That was a close encounter

Katy: Close encounter with what?..With a bear?

Alex: That's the way I was feeling..If we did not do anything..I would have felt different in their presence..But..Because something happened between us..I was feeling guilty

Katy: You worry too much Alex..Jim is not even thinking of you that way

Alex: Maybe you are right

Katy: Not maybe..I am sure that I am right..He is my husband..I know him more than anyone


_It's Friday..Frantz invites a couple friends over to have a beer or two..Nancy is not talking to him..It's a good time for him to catch up with his buddies..Frantz wants to take the opportunity to ask the guys to convince Alex to let go of that dangerous relationship he started with Jim Castillo's wife Katy


Frantz: Eric..How are you?..You look good..You've been going to the gym?

Eric: Not really..I need to get back into it..The guys are here already?

Frantz: Alex and Robert are here..They are watching the game

Robert: How are you Brother?

Eric: I am fine

Alex: Big guy..How are you?

Robert: I am ok..I wish I was doing as well as you

Alex: What do you mean?

Robert: I heard the news..The man who is walking on a thin ice

Eric: I heard different

Alex: Really..What do you hear?

Eric: I heard his new name is the walking dead

Alex: That's cold guys..You guys watch too much TV

Frantz: Guys..Let's go outside on the balcony

Eric: Frantz..Do you have the dip that you had the last time?

Frantz: No..I don't..Nancy made it for me the last time..She is not talking to me..No luck

Robert: Not talking to you..What could be wrong in paradise?

Eric: What could be wrong between Romeo and Juliet I would say?

Frantz: That guy Alex

Alex: Alex?..Don't blame me brother

Frantz: Who should I blame?..He called me on the phone hundred times while I was on my date night with Nancy..She convinced me to pick up the phone..Of course Nancy would want to know what you had to tell me after you call me more than one hundred times

Alex: C'mon man..You can't blame me for that

Robert: You are in love with your boss..There is nothing wrong with that

Frantz: There is something wrong with it..You know why..She is married..Not divorced..Not separated

Eric: Actually..Most couples meet at their workplaces..But..If she is married..I don't think it's the right relationship

Alex: Don't listen to Frantz..I don't have a relationship with her

Frantz: It does not matter how you want to call it..You are on a death row

Alex: Listen to this guy..You will think I kill someone..Pass me the pizza box Eric

Eric: But..Seriously..If she is married this is not something to do..But if she is not..This is the best romance ever..You look forward to go to work every day..She is the boss..You will not get in trouble..I think it's the best relationship

Frantz: Eric..Eric..Guys..There is one thing you guys don't understand..Not only is she married..Listen to this..She is married to the notorious Jim Castillo

Alex: Here we go

Robert: What's in that bag?

Frantz: That's wine..You guys want to drink something other than beers..I got you..You know me..I have some vodka here

Eric: Bring me some vodka..It's getting serious here

Frantz: Alex..Order some more pizza

Alex: How many boxes you guys want?

Frantz: Four large ones..Different topping..I know you Alex..You like pepperoni ..You might order all pepperoni

Alex: It's a good thing you said something..That's all I know when it comes to pizza

Frantz: Guys..Don't get too distracted here..I am trying to save this guy's life

Alex: Yep..He is my life saver

Frantz:  You might think it's funny now..But..Wait until Jim suspects that you are having an affair with his wife

Alex:  So what..I would move to Europe

Frantz:  Ok silly..You would have been in the lion den..The guy is Italian..Where do you think Italy is?..In Africa?

Alex:  Katy told me..But he does not look Italian..He is very dark

Frantz:  There are very dark Italian people..Especially the ones in Sicily..Guys..You heard of Jim Castillo?

Robert:  Yes..Of course

Eric:  Who hasn't?

Robert:  That's the guy who killed the pool guy

Alex:  C'mon guy..He did not kill the guy..The guy disappeared..Katy told me it's a rumor

Eric:  Why you guys are talking about Jim Castillo here

Frantz:  Why?..Because..The lady Alex is dating is Jim Castillo's wife

Robert:  Wait a minute?..Jim Castillo's wife is your boss?

Alex:  Yeah..I don't see why mister drama Frantz is making such a big deal about it

Eric:  This is very serious Alex..You are playing with fire here

Frantz:  She moved him inside her office

Robert:  What do you mean?

Alex:  Not a big deal..I share the office with her

Robert:  What are you going to say when her husband comes to the job?

Alex:  He was there yesterday..He did not say anything..Well..He said a couple things..He asked me to behave myself..There was another scary guy with him..Tony

Eric:  Whose phone is ringing?

Alex:  That's mine..Hello..That's her guys..Be quiet

Frantz:  That guy is so dead

Katy:  Hello..What took you so long to answer the phone?..Were you busy?

Alex:  No..I am not busy..I am just here with the guys

Katy: Who?..Frantz?

Alex: Yeah..Frantz and a couple more..Robert and Eric

Katy: How many ladies are there?

Alex: No ladies..Just me and the guys..Having beers and pizza

Katy: I bought you something..I want to bring it for you

Alex: You want to bring it to me?

Frantz: No..Not here..She is not coming to my place

Katy: I heard someone said something

Alex: Nobody said anything..But..I am far away from the workplace

Katy: Where are you?

Alex: I am at my friend's apartment..He lives on the east side of town

Katy: This is not a problem..I just finished doing my nails..I am still in the east side..That should not be a problem

Alex: But..You have other things to do..You could give it to me another time

Katy: I only have to go get my massage..I can cancel it

Alex: You don't need to do that

Katy: Are you trying to avoid me?

Alex: Not at all

Katy: Give me the address..I am on my way..I want to meet your friends anyway

Alex: It is on Park Ave..The apartment is sixteen

Katy: What is the building number?

Alex: What is the building number Frantz?

Frantz: What?..I don't know

Alex: Number twenty

Katy: I will be there soon..First..Let me talk to your friend to make sure it's ok for me to come to his place..I don't want to be the intruder

Alex: OK..Frantz..Katy wants to talk to you

Frantz: To me?..What she wants to me about?..Are you crazy?

Alex: Here

Frantz: This guy is annoying..Say I am in the bathroom

Alex: Here is the phone

Katy: Hello..Frantz

Frantz: Hello..Hi

Katy: How are you?..I wanted to ask you if it is ok to come to your place

Frantz: Sure..No problem at all

Katy: I have manners..I don't want to just come and crash your party

Frantz: You are fine..You are welcome..Number twenty and the apartment is sixteen

Katy: Thank you Frantz..See you soon

Frantz: You are welcome..See you soon

Alex: She is a nice person..Isn't she?

Frantz: Don't even talk to me dude

Alex: Guys..Did you see that..He punched me hard..What is this about bro?

Frantz: I don't want her at my place..Why you invited Jim Castillo's wife to my place

Alex: Did you hear this guy..I invited her?..You were on the phone telling her "You are welcome"..You invited her to your place..I have witnesses..Guys..Tell the truth..Didn't he invite her?

Eric: He did..This is not a big deal though

Frantz: It is a big deal..The lady is married to Jim Castillo..Why you are invited her to my place

Alex: C'mon Frantz..Don't be such a chicken..You could have told her don't come..But you chose not to..I have a feeling that you like her

Frantz: This guy will be punched in the face soon..I was nice to her on the phone because I don't want you to lose your job

Alex: Lose my job..You think she would fire me if you had told her not to come here..You must be insane..She would not hire you..But..She would not fire me for that..She is in love with me

Eric: Guys..The pizza is here

Alex: Here's the money Eric..I need to talk to this guy here

Eric: How much tip do I give him?

Alex: It does not matter..Let him keep the change..Listen bro..Don't be mad at me..You had a chance to solve the problem and you did not..So..Now..I don't want to hear it

Robert: Guys..I think she is here..She drives a baby blue Mercedes?

Alex: That's her

Frantz: Go and meet her outside dude

Alex: Dude..Don't push me..What's a matter with you?..I will punch you in your mouth

Frantz: Go outside dude

Alex: Stop pushing me..She is at the door

Katy: Hello

Frantz: Hello..Come in

Katy: Thank you..How beautiful is your place?..Wow..You decorated it yourself?

Frantz: Nancy and I did it..She did the most of it

Alex: Hello Katy

Katy: Hi honey

Alex: This is Eric..And this is Robert..You know Frantz..Right?

Katy: I don't know Frantz..I just met him..Right now

Alex: You know what I mean..You spoke with him on the phone

Katy: Nice to meet you Frantz..Thank you for letting me into your place..It seems that I am chasing this guy all over town..Doesn't it guys?

Eric: No..Not at all

Frantz: Have a seat please

Katy: Thank you..I can't stay too long

Frantz: Why is that..You just got here?

Katy: My husband is on that new thing..He put a GPS in my car to track my way around

Frantz: He did?

Katy: Just for fun

Frantz: You mean..Right now..He would know where you are?

Katy: Certainly

Frantz: Eric..Pass me the vodka please

Katy: Are you ok?

Frantz: I am fine

Katy: You act as if you've seen a ghost..He does not do it in any malicious way..When I get home he will tell me..Honey you were there..You stopped there..Just for fun

Robert: I see

Katy: Like I said guys.. I can't stay..Another time I will stay longer..By the way your friend is such a great guy..Great worker

Robert: He is kind of lazy

Katy: Not at all..If I ask him to stay late..He will gladly do it

Robert: Who wouldn't?

Katy: What do you mean?

Robert: You seem so nice..I wish my boss was as nice as you are

Katy: Thank you Robert..It seems I have a new friend..You are so nice Robert..Can I borrow your friend Alex for a minute guys?

Frantz: Sure..Take him away

Katy: He will be back soon

Alex: Alright guys..See you soon..You see my phone anywhere?

Eric: It's on the kitchen table

Alex: See you guys

Frantz: Dude you are dead..Jim will kill you

Alex: You are just hating

Robert: Damn..She is so fine

Eric: I did not know she was that fine..Frantz needs to shut up

Alex: I told y'all

Katy: I forgot to say goodbye to them..Bye Frantz..Bye guys

Frantz: Bye Katy

Eric: Come back anytime

Frantz: Dude..Anytime where?

Eric: I was just being nice..Listen brother..We can't lie..She is fine

Robert: Oh my god..Fine is an understatement

Frantz: Jim will kill all of you

Robert: This is worth dying for..What do you think Eric?

Eric: For sure..Dying?..Bury me alive

Frantz: You guys are a bunch of fools..I just don't want to be involved when things are getting heated..Too many times I found myself involved in some nonsense because of Alex..Since elementary school..Always some guys waiting for him after school..And he is waiting for me to help him fight

Robert: I know

Frantz: One time..They were waiting for him..He came to tell me..I told him why you are telling me for..I said..Go and fight them..He got some nerves to tell me hurry up..Now as an adult..I am not going to fight Jim Castillo's Klan for you my friend..You can forget about that..There is no fighting Jim Castillo anyway..Alex will be dead soon..The guy has a GPS in his wife car..He is now in the man's wife's car driving around..He is a dead man

Eric: You have a point here..All jokes aside..He did not put the GPS in her car for no reason

Robert: Of course not..He might make her believe it's for fun..But..In fact..He is watching

Frantz: Of course..I feel sorry for Alex..He is so naïve

Eric: You are already involved..If there is a GPS in the car..Jim will know that she stopped here at your place

Frantz: No doubt..No doubt at all

Eric: You should move Frantz

Frantz: It would not be a bad idea


_Meanwhile


Katy: Do you think your friends know there is something between us?

Alex: They might..They are not stupid

Katy: You are a kiss and tell guy Alex..Aren't you?..You told them everything..How embarrassing..If I had known that..I would not have come inside..You did tell them..Didn't you?

Alex: No..I did not..You told them

Katy: How so?

Alex: I said hello to you..You kissed me right on my lips..And said..Hi honey

Katy: The kiss was an accident..I did not mean to kiss your lips

Alex: Then you said..Hi honey

Katy: I forgot..I think I am falling in love with you

Alex: Katy..Remember..We can't take it deeper than what it is right now..There is no falling in love..You are trying to get me killed here

Katy: By whom?..By my husband?..I promise you if he kills you I will kill him

Alex: This is a promise I don't want you to keep..We have to be more careful

Katy: More careful?..And you already told all your friends..Wait..My phone is ringing..This is yours

Alex: No Katy..It's your phone

Katy: Hello

Giselle: Hello..Where are you?..I stopped at your house..Jim told me you went for some errands..Since when you do errands?

Katy: I know right?..I am with my prince charmant

Giselle: What is name again?

Katy: Why you want to know his name Giselle?

Alex: Don't tell people my name

Giselle: I think I know him

Katy: You don't know him Giselle..From where?

Giselle: His name is Alain?

Katy: No..He is not Alain

Giselle: Where are you heading?

Katy: Just driving around

Giselle: You know Jim has a GPS in your car..You have to be careful

Katy: Tell me about it..I will call you later when I get home

Giselle: Be careful..You know Jim will kill you if he finds out that you are messing around

Katy: He is worth dying for

Giselle: Really?..It's that deep?

Katy: It is even deeper than that

Giselle: We need to talk girlfriend..When can we talk Katy?

Katy: I will call you when I get home

Giselle: No..Not that kind of talk..I need to be in your face kind of talk..I need to wake you up..Because.. You are talking crazy..You know Jim would kill you if he finds out that you are messing around with that guy..In fact he will kill both of you

Katy: I got this..I got everything under control

Giselle: You don't sound like it..Next weekend we go out for dinner

Katy: No problem..You are taking away my precious time here..Bye Giselle..I love you

Alex: Where are we going babe?

Katy:  Let's go to the office

Alex: Alright

Katy: Is this a light in my office?

Alex: It's the reflection of the streets light

Katy: Ok..Come..I want you so much

Alex:  Babe..You are dragging me

Katy:  Walk..Walk faster

Alex:  It's dark here

Katy:  I could not wait to be alone with you..Oh my god

Alex:  Your body is so warm

Katy:  Oh my god..It feels s good

Alex:  Your phone is ringing

Katy:  Oh my god it's Jim..Be quiet

Jim:  Hello

Katy:  Hi honey

Jim:  The GPS is showing that you are at work

Katy:  I was driving by and I saw a light on..I came to turn it off..Don't move..I will scream babe

Alex: It's so good

Katy: Ugh..Ah

Jim:  Did you say something?

Katy:  No..No..I am fine..I hit my hand in the door knob

Jim:  Listen to me Katy..You have to be careful..Since you found the light on..There could be an intruder in the building

Katy:  No..I don't think so..I will be fine

Jim:  Listen..I am not too far from the office..I will be there in five to seven minutes or so

Katy:  You should not..I am fine

Alex: What's going on?

Katy: He is on his way here

Alex: Here where?

Katy: Here..Here..On his way to the office

Jim:  I am on my way see you soon

Katy: Ok..Ok

Alex: What is going on?

Katy: Go..Go..Leave..Jim is on his way here

Alex: Are you serious?

Katy: More serious than a heart attack..Leave now

Alex: Where do I go?..I could hide in another room

Katy: No..This is not a good idea..He thinks there is an intruder in the building..Therefore he might search the rooms

Alex: You are right

Katy: Go through the back..Hurry up

Alex: Are you going to be alright?

Katy: Yes..Go..Go


_A few minutes later


Jim: Honey..Where are you?

Katy: I am here in the bathroom

Jim: Are you ok?..You seem agitated..And sweating lightly

Katy: Yes..You really scared me when you said there could be an intruder..I was hiding in there..It's hot in there..This is why I am sweating a bit

Jim: Let me check the rooms..Who those socks belongs to?

Katy: What are you talking about?..Oh those..They must be Alex..He is such a slab..They must have dropped from his gym bag

Jim: You need to remind him that this is not his bedroom

Katy: I know..I know honey..I will speak to him..Do you want something to drink?

Jim: No..Let me check the other rooms very quickly

_Meanwhile..Frantz's phone is ringing

Frantz: Hello

Alex: Frantz..Where is Eric?

Frantz: He left..What's going on?

Alex: Where is Robert?

Frantz: They are both gone..What do you want?..Are you running..You seem to be out of breath

Alex: I was trying to move away from the area

Frantz: What area?..What are you talking about?

Alex: My job..The office

Frantz: Are you ok..Where is Katy?..I thought you were with Katy..Where is she?

Alex: I left her at the office

Frantz: I don't understand

Alex: Listen Frantz..I want you to do me a big favor bro

Frantz: What favor?

Alex: I want you to come pick me up..I need a ride to get away from the area as quick as possible

Frantz: Why?..What is wrong?

Alex: I was in the office with Katy..And Jim decided to come by..Come get me out of here bro

Frantz: Man..You must be crazy..Call someone else..I told you about this..I told you that I was not going to be involved in this mess..Bye

Alex: Wait..Wait

Frantz: Why are you calling my phone dude?.. What again brother?

Alex: C'mon brother..Don't be stupid.. I can't walk all the way home from downtown..Beside..Jim knows what I look like

Frantz: Tough luck..Wrap your head with your shirt or something..So he does not recognize you

Alex: This is not funny..This is no time to joke..Hold on there is car coming..Let me get out of the way..It could be him

Frantz: Don't get out of the way..Put your thumb out..You might get a r de..If it Jim..It will be even better..Because you met him already

Alex: Bro..Stop playing..Damn

Frantz: What happened?..He saw you?

Alex: I just realized that I left my socks on the floor

Frantz: On the floor where?

Alex: In the office

Frantz: Why you had your socks off dude?

Alex: I like to be completely naked during love making

Frantz: I see..And you like to be fully dressed when you are running from a killer husband

Alex: This is not funny..Come get me..I will pay you back bro

Frantz: This is how I want you to pay me back..I am going to risk my life and pick you up..Not for you..Just because I know your family..Especially your mom..They are good people..They don't deserve to be at your funeral now..But..I want you to pay me back by not talking to me anymore..By staying out of my life..I am not going to keep on fighting for you like I did in high schoo  bro..I am at the verge of losing my girlfriend because of you

Alex: I agree..I won't talk to you ever again..I won't come to your place..Come pick me up bro..Hurry up

Frantz: Hurry up?..I am not UBER dude

Alex: Hurry up already..Stop playing Frantz


_Ten minutes later


Alex: Thanks man

Frantz: Didn't I tell you not to talk to me dude..Just be quiet..Now you see what I was talking about..The storm called Jim is knocking at your door..You get what you wanted

Alex: Bro if you only knew..She is so sweet

Frantz: I don't want to hear it

Alex: Dude..I mean she has skills..The best ever

Frantz:  Just a minute ago..You were begging me to come here and pick you up..You were as scared as a mouse at a cat's funeral..Now..You can't stop running your mouth

Alex:  I just want to share the experience with you..My phone is ringing..That's Robert

Robert:  Hey playboy..How was it?

Alex:  Everything went fine..The best ever

Frantz:  Did you say everything went fine..Give me that damn phone

Alex:  Dude..This is my phone..What's a matter with you?

Frantz:  Robert..This is guy here was crying like a baby

Robert:  Really?..What happened?

Frantz:  Jim walked up on him while he was with Katy

Robert:  Are you serious?

Frantz:  This is why he is in my car..I had to come and pick his sorry self up..He was crying

Alex:  Give me my phone bro..Listen Robert..You know me better than that..I am not afraid of Jim..Frantz is the one making a big deal about that guy

Robert:  He is not making a big deal about the guy..That's the guy's wife you are messing with

Alex:  I know..What am I supposed to do..She likes me..I am not married..I am single

Robert:  I got your point..You are not married..The responsibility should have been hers to respect her marriage

Alex:  Exactly

Robert:  But..That does not put you on the right..You do have some level of responsibility as well..If she was not married..Even if she was just dating that guy..I will give you a pass..But..She is married

Frantz:  Yep..Remind him who she is married to Robert

Robert:  That's Frantz talking

Alex:  Yeah..You are on speaker..He can hear you

Robert:  Like I said..It's very tempting..She looks great

Frantz:  I know..But..The risk of dying is greater

Alex:  Hey Bob..Let me call you later..She is on the other line

Frantz:  Here we go..He is dead Bob..Get your funeral suit ready

Alex:  Quiet Frantz..Hello..Hi

Katy:  Hello..How are you..Are you ok?..I was worried sick

Alex:  I am fine

Katy:  How did you make it out?

Alex:  My buddy Frantz came to pick me up

Katy:  That's so cute..He is so nice

Alex:  That's my best buddy

Frantz:  Shut the hell up

Katy:  What did he say?

Alex:  I think he said hell yeah

Katy:  It was so good

Alex:  What did you love the most about it?

Katy:  Everything..The thrill of it was crazy..I like the thrill of almost getting caught

Alex:  You can talk..Are you sure he cannot hear you?

Katy:  No..Not at all..I am all the way at the other end of the house..It's a bit bigger than your friend's apartment

Alex:  My friend's apartment is a nice size though

Katy:  This is a sixteen bedrooms house..When I say I am at the other end I really mean it

Alex:  I see..You might need a cab to travel to the other side

Katy:  Exactly

Frantz:  What about my apartment..Nobody is coming to my place

Alex:  Shut up dude

Katy:  I miss you already..I wish that Jim did not have to come there..We were having the best time..Weren't we?

Alex:  Yes..Listen..I left my socks on the floor..I hope Jim did not see it

Katy: He did too

Alex: Are you serious?

Katy: Honey..I would not lie about this..In fact..I don't lie at all..This is why when I told you that I love you..I really mean it

Alex: Whatever Katy..You already know we cannot take this to the next level..What did he say about the socks?

Katy: He asked me whose socks..I told him they must be yours..They must have fallen from your gym bag

Alex: What did he say?

Katy: Why you want to know everything he said?

Alex: I have to know..To figure out whether he suspects something

Katy: And..If he did..You will leave the country?

Alex: Stop playing Katy

Katy: He did not say anything..Jim trusts me..He loves me..He believes everything I say to him

Alex: So..Let me ask you this..Why are you cheating on him?

Katy: I am not cheating on him..I am just having fun with you..This is not cheating..This is my own body..And I think I can have fun if I want to

Alex: But..You are his wife..It's not like you are dating him

Katy: I know..I am still married to him..I am still his wife..I just want to have some fun..I like the thrill of it..The danger that is involved in doing this

Alex: You like the danger?

Katy: Yes..It feels so good..When he said that he was coming to the office yesterday..That was the best feeling ever..It's like going down upside down on a roller coaster

Alex: Well..This is not a game..If we get caught doing it..The situation can get really complicated..I am not afraid of him..I will defend myself..But..This is not something we should look forward to

Katy: You would fight him?..He does not fight people..He let his friend Tony do the dirty work for him

Alex: Who's Tony?..The guy I saw the other day?

Katy: He is a tough guy

Alex: He is kind of big..But I fought guys that were way bigger than him

Frantz: With my help..Or..You would not be here..You realized that we are here in front of your place..Get out already

Alex: Chill man

Katy: What do you say?

Alex: Nothing..I meant to ask you something..You don't mind..Right?

Katy: What?..Ask me

Alex: First..I want to congratulate you

Katy: On what?

Alex: On your skills

Katy: What are you talking about?

Alex: You have knowledge

Katy: Oh my god..You are so funny..You are making me blush..Your friend is listening..Stop talking like that

Alex: You said that you don't mind dirty talk..Right?

Katy: Not in front of your friend..That's embarrassing

Alex: He is ok with it

Frantz: Dude don't get me involved in your stuffs

Katy: I heard him talking..What did he say?

Alex: He said he is all for the dirty talk

Katy: Really?..This is so embarrassing

Frantz: Dude..Shut up..Stop playing

Alex: Let me ask you a question Katy

Katy: Go right ahead

Alex: Do you love your husband?

Katy: Why you asked?

Alex: I am just curious

Katy: I do love him..Very much

Alex: But you said the other day that you love me..You were playing..Weren't you?

Katy: No..I was not playing..I love my husband and I love you as well..Is that strange?

Alex: No..But

Katy: But what?..Society tries to put in our head that we supposed to love one person..In fact we all know that you can have feelings for other people even when you are married or involved in a relationship..Let's be honest Alex..How many relationships have you been in

Alex: I can't count..Ten..Eleven..Even more

Katy: Ok..You told all those women that you loved them..Right?

Alex: I guess

Katy: Not I guess..Answer me..Yes or no

Alex: Yes..I think so

Katy: Ok..Therefore..We are allowed to love many people one at a time?..If you loved Julie..You loved Monique at a different time each..You can love both at the same time..What is the difference..Tell me?

Alex: You have a point here

Katy: This is that hypocrisy that society put in our head..All men want to sleep with another woman other than his wife..He woke up to same damn face every day..Sometimes the woman does not even care about her look anymore after marriage..This is just being human

Alex: I hear you..You have a point

Katy: Me..I can careless what people think..If I have feelings for someone I will go for it..For instance..I have feelings for a guy called Alex..I let him know

Alex: I know..And he is happy about it too..Those are dangerous feelings

Katy: What make them so dangerous?

Alex: Because you are married to Jim Castillo

Katy: Most men and women who are married sleep with people at their jobs

Alex: You think so?

Katy: Of course they do..They are human..One can ignore the fact as much as they want..Or be in denial as much as they want..But..That's the fact

Alex: I see..You have a strange way of thinking

Katy: Why you call it strange..Not strange at all..I am simply telling the truth

Alex: I am not denying it that men and women do feel for other people..Even when they are in a committed relationship

Katy: Listen Alex..Marriage is a man made practice..It is not a natural one..There are societies where the men are allowed to marry more than one woman..Up to six seven wives

Alex: I have to go to that country..Where is that?

Katy: Don't tell me you never hear of polygamy societies..There are some even right here in America

Alex: I have to polygamize myself

Katy: Stop being funny Alex..Polygamize is not a word

Alex: It is not?..Sorry..Well they better make it a good one because that's what I want to be..Polygamized

Katy: Very funny..This is why I like talking to you..You always make me laugh

Alex: Are you sure that's the only reason?

Katy: What other reason?

Alex: I thought it was deeper than that?

Katy: Nope..That's the only reason..I think it's deep enough

Alex: You think making you laugh is deep enough?

Katy: Sure..That's all I want..People often complicate stuff..If a guy can make you laugh all the time..That's happiness right there..Nothing can replace that..Money..Jewelry..No material things can replace that..When you find a guy that can make you laugh..Keep him

Alex: Are you talking to me?..I don't need a guy

Katy: Silly..You know what I mean..If you find a girl that makes you laugh keep her..Like me..I do make you laugh..Don't I?

Alex: I don't know about that

Katy: Really?..I am so hurt right now

Alex: I am only kidding..You make me feel good..I mean..You do make me feel good

Katy: You like the way I do?

Alex: It's so good..I think you should patent it..No wonder your husband is crazy about you

Katy: All the men I have been with were crazy about me

Alex: Where do you get all this knowledge?

Katy: I was born this way..It's all in my head

Alex: Tell me about it

Frantz: Dude..Bring you a pillow or something..You are not going to get out of my car?

Katy: Who is talking to you?

Alex: Who else?..My hater friend

Katy: Frantz?

Alex: Yep

Frantz: Brother..Are you nuts?..You put the seat in my car all the way back like it is yours.. And talking to that woman like she is yours..You have something coming

Frantz: He is complaining because I put the seat in his car all the way back while talking to you..I want to be comfortable while talking to you..Are you sitting or lying down?

Katy: I am lying down on a long chair

Frantz: What do you have on?

Katy: Just underwear..Why you are asking..Are you coming?

Alex: I would love to

Katy: We have to do that sometimes..I will let you know..I will take you in to visit my house..You will love it

Alex: I don't think it's a safe idea to come to your house

Katy: Why not?..Trust me..I know all the hiding places in this house

Alex: You are topless..Just with underwear..You are not worried about the neighbors

Katy: What neighbors..My closest neighbor is my friend Marlene..She is two football fields away

Alex: You seem to be very comfortable with your birthday suit

Katy: Totally

Alex: Do you go to the gym?..How do you maintain this figure?

Katy: I don't go to the gym..It is natural..I had a nice body since I was thirteen years old..It's hereditary..I am Italian..Hispanic and Black

Alex: Ok..No wonder you are so fine..It's a United Nations kind of thing..Or united ethnicities I should say

Katy: It's a multi racial kind of thing baby

Alex: I love it..My friends think you look good

Frantz: Hey..Be specific dude

Katy: Who..Frantz..Robert and Eric?

Alex: Robert and Eric

Katy: Frantz did not like the way I look?

Alex: He did

Katy: Hold on..I think Jim is looking for me..I heard him buzzing

Alex: You have a buzzer?

Katy: Yes..This place is so huge..We will never find each other..When he buzzes me..I know exactly where he is in the house..I can also talk to him..Let me see what he wants

Alex: No problem

Katy: Hi honey

Jim: Where are you?

Katy: I am outside on the balcony..What do you want?..You need me?

Jim: Where is my box of cigars?

Katy: Honey..You have so many of them..Look in the kitchen down stairs..You have some in our bedroom as well

Jim: What are you doing outside..Aren't you cold?

Katy: You know I love the cold..I am on the phone with my friend

Jim: The lady is leaving..She prepared dinner..You come and eat if you are hungry

Katy: Thanks my love..I am not hungry yet..Bye

Alex: Are you in trouble?

Katy: Me?.. No..Not at all..I am spoiled..My husband spoiled me..He was looking for his cigars..And He wanted me to come and eat dinner..The chef prepared dinner

Alex: You have a chef too?

Katy: Of course..It's good to have a chef..You don't have to think of what to eat all the time..She thinks and cooks it..And it's healthier than what I would cook anyway

Alex: I do have a chef as well

Katy: Oh..You do?

Alex: Yep..His name is McDonald

Katy: You are so silly..He used to be my chef for a long time too

Alex: How could you spend so much time away from your husband?

Katy: I like it..This is why I like the big house..We are not on top of each other..I brought a bottle of wine out and some grapes..And I am fine..I don't want to see him until it's time to go to bed

Alex: He does not miss you..If my wife was that fine..I will live in the smallest house so I could be on top of her all the time..Twenty four seven

Katy: You are too funny..He does not like that..He likes to spend time with his friends..He was asking for his cigars..I know his friends are coming over..They are going to play poker

Alex: He plays poker..I have to come and show him my poker skills

Katy: I don't think you will last on that table..I saw those guys making million dollars bid

Alex: You mean million..Real money?

Katy: No Alex..Monopoly money

Alex: Ok..You are being funny..I see you

Katy: Not at all..You said real money..The only other money I know beside real ones is monopoly


_Meanwhile.. Downstairs in the game room


Jim: Have a seat guys..Tony..I thought you said you could not make it

Tony: I was supposed to go out with my wife..She said she is not feeling too well

Jim:  Look who is here tonight..Joey

Joey:  How you doing Jim?

Tony:  He came with a pocket full of money

Jim:  He better..Because last time he cleaned the table..I want some of my money back.. Jimmy..Bring a couple more bottles on the table for me..Al..Remove your gun off the table

Tony:  Jim..The guy is a black guy..You know he does not go anywhere without a gun

Al:  That is so not true..I only bring my gun because I don't trust you guys

Tony:  Al..We know each other for more than twenty five years..Right Jim?

Jim:  Al is a maniac..Paranoid

Al:  Whatever..I just don't trust you guys with my money

Jim:  By the way..He brought a trunk full of lobsters for me today

Al:  Very expensive stuff Jim..You owe me

Jim:  Frankie..Don't be shy..Help yourself..Have a drink..Those are the most expensive bottles I have in the house

Tony:  Frankie..Don't fall for that..He is trying to get you drunk early..Then he will get in your pocket

Jim:  Tony..How could you say such a thing about me..You know how much I love the guy

Tony:  I am always careful around this guy

Jim:  Listen kids..I have something to tell you guys

Jimmy:  What is it?

Jim:  I have a feeling that something is happening

Tony:  Something is always happening somewhere..You haven't said anything yet Jim..What is matter with you?  Are you drunk already?

Jim:  No..No..This is no joke..I think my wife is doing something

Tony:  Yes..She is talking on the phone..Who are you talking about..You are not talking about my girl Katy..Are you?

Jim:  Yes..In think she is seeing someone

Frankie: Jim..Why would you say such a thing..She will leave you if she finds out about what you just said there

Jim: Listen guy..It's a feeling that I have

Tony: I know what it is..You just ran out of Viagra..Didn't you Jim?

Jim: Guys..All jokes aside..I was not born yesterday

Tony: We all know that..This is why we think you should restock on your Viagra and stop blaming our girl

Jim: I am not blaming her

Tony: It is worse than blaming her..You are accusing her of being a cheater..You know a lot of guys got shot by their wives jut for that

Al: Guys..Let the man explain himself

Jim: Guys..It's a gut feeling that I have..A couple things happened that made me believe she could be messing around

Frankie: Like what Jim?

Jim: She has been pretty distant lately

Tony: Jim..From the time I know you guys..You guys are always apart..Away from each other..I guess that's the way you wanted it..This is why you bought such a huge place

Jim: You are right about that..I don't want her to be on top of me

Frankie: Listen to this guy...You have to love your wife being on top of you

Jim: You know what I mean

Tony: Pass me the cognac please..And who do you think she is messing around with?

Jim: There is a guy at the office

Tony: That kid we met the other day?

Jim: I think something is happening

Tony: I don't think he is foolish enough to do such a thing..He seem s to be a smart kid

Jim: Well..My wife moved him inside her office

Tony: I did not see anything wrong with that

Jim:  Wait..I am shaving you..You are touching it..You are going to get cut..The other night..You know I have a GPS in my wife Mercedes..Right? So..She made two unusual stops..She stopped at an address..I don't think she has any friend in that building..Then she went to the office

Tony:  She went to the office?

Frankie:  Are you serious?

Jim:  I am not making this up

Tony:  Jim..This cognac is the best..Where did you find it?

Jim:  My brother sent it to me..Listen now kids..This is serious..I called her..I asked her what you are doing at the office..She said that she was driving by and saw a light on..She went in to turn it off

Tony:  So far..I don't see anything that would make you suspect her of cheating on you

Jim:  Wait a minute..It gets better..While I was in there..At the office..She seemed a little agitated..Then I looked on the floor and I saw a pair of socks

Jonny:  What do you mean by pair of socks

Frankie:  Jim..This is not something to play with..You are trying to get the kid kill here

Jim:  I am not kidding..I saw a pair of man socks on the floor

Tony:  What explanation she gave you regarding those socks?

Jim:  She said they are Alex's socks

Jonny: Who is Alex?

Tony:  C'mon Jonny we don't have all day..Keep going Jim

Jim:  Alex is the guy who works at the office..This is the one I think that my wife is messing around with..So when I asked her whose socks..She said they belong to Alex..And they had fallen from his gym bag

Tony:  You should have picked them up and smelled them..At least check to see if they are warm

Frankie:  What did you say Tony?

Jonny:  Tony is crazy

Frantz:  And nasty too

Jim:  What do you guys think of it?

Frankie: Nothing..You need to have real proof before you even talk about something like that..Don't even tell that story to anyone else..They will think that you lack confidence..You are Jim..Jim Castillo..And you know that kind of talk can get the kid killed

Tony: You are right about that Frankie..Some guys will kill the kid just to please you..You should not talk about it anymore comprende?..Now ..Let's make some money..I have a pocket full of money here..And you are wasting time talking about some guys you think is sleeping with your wife

Jonny: You know what the problem is..She is too beautiful..She is driving you crazy

Jim: What I should do about it

Frankie: Shoot him Jim..What do you want me to tell you? Nothing..You should not do anything

Tony: If it really bothers you?..Go ahead and put a private instigator to watch what is going on

Jim: This is not a bad idea..Al..You are quiet about it..What do you think?

Al: I don't know..My woman knows better than that..I don't think about those situations

Jim: What would you do..If you walk in your home and find your lady with another guy..You would shoot him..Wouldn't you Al

Al: Not really..I am not about to spend my life in prison for thing like that..One guy is dead and another is in prison..You are both gone..The woman finds another man

Jonny: Al has a good point here..If you want I can get you a private investigator

Tony: You know Jonny has all kind of connection..I think he is working for the Fed

Jonny: I am not a rat..But..My cousin Antonio is a private instigator

Tony: Is he? And you never said anything..He is always inside my house

Jonny: He is no rat..He is a good guy..I will tell him about it

Jim: Tell him to call me

Frankie: Jim..You are really serious about that..Aren't you?

Jim: My gut feeling does not deceive me..I have a feeling something is happening..For instance right now she is outside talking on the phone..She has been on the phone for more than an hour

Frankie: C'mon Jim..She talks on the phone all the times..Sometimes my wife talks on the phone with her for hours

Jim: I know..But..This is different..She has a bottle of wine out there..She is topless..She is wearing only panties

Tony: I know Jim for a long time..I think he worries about it..Jonny..Tomorrow send your cousin here to talk to him

Jonny: I can call him right now if you want to

Tony: Call him then


_Meanwhile upstairs on the balcony


Katy: I want to see you so bad..I feel like going out and meet you

Alex: No..No Katy..I don't think it's a good idea..I think Jim might suspect something..We need to slow down a bit..We almost got caught at the office..I really think that Jim might suspect something

Katy: You don't know Jim the way I do..He is my husband..I don't think he suspects anything

Alex: Some men play this very well..They will act as if they don't suspect just to watch and see what is going on

Katy: He is a very busy guy..He does not have time for that

Alex: Love makes a man do crazy things sometimes

Katy: Let me give you some good news

Alex: What good news?

Katy: Jim is going away two days from now..He is going to Europe for business..I think it's the perfect time to bring you in

Alex: What do you mean?

Katy:  To bring you inside my home..I just want you to visit my place

Alex: This is an exciting and also scary thought..Who's going to be there?

Katy: It's basically me and the chef..Also a security guy..I will call the security firm..He does not report to Jim..I will hire him when Jim leaves

Alex: You mean there will be no one to snitch about me coming there

Katy: Correct..I need you to trust me a little

Alex: I do trust you..But we also have to be careful

Katy: Are you going to come or not?

Alex: I don't see why not..Listen Katy..My buddy here is looking at me like he is about to stab me in my neck..He was on his phone all that time..Now he is paying attention to us talking

Katy: He's been waiting for a long time..Get out of his car already

Alex: I know..Talk to you tomorrow

Katy: What is tomorrow?..Sunday?

Katy: I will talk to you..Maybe I will pass by your place to see you

Alex: Bye

Katy: I love you

Alex: Bye

Katy: You did not hear me?..I said I love you

Alex: Oh..Thank you

Katy: What do you mean thank you?..This is not what you say..That's all you have to say?..Thank you?

Alex: Oh..I love you too

Katy: Is it so hard to say?..You don't love me do you Alex?

Alex: I do..But..It very dangerous for you..I don't want you to get hurt or destroy your marriage

Katy: You worry too much..Let me worry about my marriage..Can you just relax and have some fun

Alex: Sure I can

Katy: Ok..So..This week..My husband is leaving for a trip to Europe..I want you to come and spend a couple nights with me

Alex: Couple nights?..I definitely will come..But..Don't know how many nights I will spend there

Katy: Don't be a chicken..I will make my chef prepare you the best meals..And we will have the finest drinks..I forgot to mention that you will also have me..It will be just like being in paradise

Alex: That's not a bad definition of paradise at all

Katy: See..Paradise will be waiting for you

Alex: I am looking forward to it

Katy: Night..Night my love

Alex:  Good night babe

Frantz:  Dude..I just realized that you have a death wish..You are calling Jim's wife babe..Good night babe?..Are you crazy?

Alex:  Dude..You don't understand..She is in love..That's the finest woman I ever had

Frantz:  It's going to be the best funeral you ever had

Alex:  C'mon brother..Don't be so pessimistic..Next week Jim will be out of town..She invited me to come over

Frantz:  To come over where?

Alex:  To her house..It's only one life to live my friend..You have to have fun

Frantz:  You can have calculated fun

Alex:  Calculated fun?..How can it be fun if it is calculated?

Frantz:  Well..Fun that is not calculated can lead you to be six feet under..And I think that's exactly where this one is taking you

Alex:  It seems like you are getting ready for my funeral already?

Frantz:  Getting ready?..Are you kidding me?..I have my outfit and all

Alex:  That's so not cool brother..You are planning my funeral without telling me?

Frantz:  I never said that I was planning your funeral..All I am saying is..I am getting ready

Alex:  You are going to wait a long time


_A week later


Jim:  Babe..I am leaving this morning

Katy:  I am going to miss you so much..How long you will stay?

Jim:  I will spend the whole week

Katy:  I thought you were coming back Thursday?

Jim:  No..My cousin is getting married in Italy..So..I Have to be at the wedding..This is why I wanted you to go with me..You could go to the wedding with me and meet them

Katy: I met them last time we were there

Jim: You did?..I don't remember

Katy: Yes I did..The one with the big mustache..Joey

Jim: Yes..Joey..He is the one getting married

Katy: When are you coming back?

Jim: Next Monday..Just be good..Ok?

Katy: C'mon Jim..I am always good

Jim: I have to get going babe..The driver is here

Katy: See you honey..Say hello to the familia for me

Jim: You should have gone with me..At this time the weather in Italy is wonderful

Katy: C'mon babe..I have been going to Italy since I was a baby..Twice every year..Once with my parents..And once with mom and dad..Every year..Bye honey

Jim: Bye..Just be good..Take good care of the place..No strangers in my home

Katy: C'mon babe..Go..You are going to be late..Did you get the gift I bought for them?

Jim: No..I don't think so

Katy: C'mon Jim..Where is your head?

Jim: I haven't been myself lately


_Jim left for his trip to Europe..Later that day..Katy meets with a couple of her friends for lunch..Let's go in with her guys and listen to the conversation..It's getting good and dangerous..Isn't it my loving readers?..We love it..Follow me


Katy: Hello

Giselle: Hello

Katy: I am in front of the place already..I don't see your car

Giselle: Do you see Martine's car?

Katy: What she is driving?

Giselle: I don't know..She has too many cars..I could not tell you..She is probably in her black corvette..That's her new toy

Katy: Well..How long until you get here Giselle?..You are always late

Giselle: I am on my way..I had to do something for my man

Katy: I thought he was not in town?

Giselle: Your man is never in town..Mine stays with me

Katy: Lucky you..Jim is always traveling..What can I do..That's part of his job..He takes good care of me

Giselle: Mine takes good care of me too

Katy: C'mon..You want to talk about spoiled..You are so spoiled..I work fulltime every day..I don't know how you do it Giselle..I would have been bored to death staying at home every day..I think I saw Martine

Giselle: She is there?

Katy: I saw her..She saw me..Look at her smiling..That's a nice car she has there..Jim better gets me one just like that

Giselle: You know how much this thing cost?..A fortune..I would rather buy a house

Katy: Really?

Giselle: Yes..It is a special edition..They are not out yet..That thing cost two hundred thousand dollars

Katy: I want one

Giselle: Good luck

Katy: She is here..We are going in

Giselle: Go ahead..I am almost there..Get the table that I like or I am leaving

Katy: You might as well make a u-turn right now Giselle..If you wanted to pick table you would have gotten here on time

Giselle: Whatever K..I am almost there


_Inside the restaurant


Katy: Look how pretty she is Giselle?

Martine: Me?..Thanks..I have been so busy lately..I don't even have time to take care of myself

Katy: You don't need to take care of yourself..I think your man is taking good care of you

Martine: Look who is talking

Giselle: Exactly..Miss spoiled

Katy: Spoiled?..I am the only one at this table with a full time job..You guys don't work

Martine: Excuse me..Talk for yourself lady

Katy: Well..You have a restaurant..That's not work Martine..You have people doing the work for you

Martine: You have the wrong idea about restaurant my dear..If you have a restaurant and you are not part of the management..I mean hands on..It will not last two weeks..I work so hard..Some weekends..I stayed on my feet for twelve hours straight

Katy: Really?

Martine: Yes..Really

Giselle: Not for me..I would die..I am allergic to working hard..And my husband knows it..Before I married him..I told him that I wanted to be a princess..And he agreed

Martine: Before I opened the restaurant..I used to stay at home..But..I started to get so bored and annoyed..I had to do something

Katy: You went t school for that too..Right?

Martine: Of course..I wanted to know at least have an idea of every aspect of the business..I earned my money

Katy: Me too

Giselle: What do you guys mean?..I don't earn mine..Really?

Giselle: I am taking care of my husband and the two children..I f this is not work I don't know what is

Katy: We need to give her credit for that..Taking care of children is the hardest thing ever

Martine: I don't have any yet..And I am not in a rush

Katy: Me either..Now it's that time to look good and have fun

Giselle: I think you are having too much fun

Katy: Stop already..I haven't even started yet

Giselle: Really?..I think you are too deep into it..Martine..Don't you think she is too deep into the fun?

Martine: I do

Katy: Do what?..Did you tell Martine what I told you?

Giselle: I did not know it was supposed to be a secret

Katy: Giselle..Stop acting dumb..Why don't you go on the radio and announce it for the whole town to know..You want Jim to kill me

Giselle: Relax..I only told Martine and a couple people at my job

Katy: Couple of people?

Giselle: I am kidding..I am kidding..I did not know you were so scared?

Katy: I am not afraid..But I just don't want my husband to find out

Martine: Are you getting in love with that guy?.Because Giselle told me that you are talking about love..This is why I decided to come here to put some sense in your head before Jim put lead in it

Katy: Whatever..Where is Jim now..He is in his way to Europe..What am I supposed to do?..Just sit pretty and waiting for him to come back

Giselle: Yes..That's what you suppose to do..Just sit pretty and wait for him to come back

Katy: Where did you guys see that?..It's not in my marriage vow..To sit pretty and wait..This is not me at all..I think I would divorce him before I become that

Giselle: I think you should divorce him before you start to sleep with someone else

Katy: Is it that kind of meeting this is going to be?..Tell me..I can move to another table

Martine: We will move right behind you

Giselle: When you are moving to another table just take my bag with you..I will be right over there

Katy: Guys..This is not funny..This is my life..I do whatever I want

Giselle: I understand this is your life Katy..But..You decided to be married..There are certain rules that go with that

Martine: Try to understand Kat..We are not trying to bust your bubble..This is a very dangerous thing you embarked on..So..You satisfied your fantasy..I think you should let go of it now

Katy: What fantasy?..I am not trying to satisfy any fantasy

Giselle: The fantasy that a lot of women have

Martine:  To experience cheating on their husbands..Some do it for the thrill..The risk that is involved

Katy:  I am not doing it for none of that

Giselle:  Why are you doing it?

Katy:  I can even explain..The thrill is part of it..But it's more than that

Martine:  What are you saying?..You love that guy?

Katy:  Maybe..I don't know how to call it..I feel good when I am with him..I feel good when I hear his voice..He is my new motivation to go to the office in the morning

Giselle:  You are traveling a very dangerous road lady

Katy:  What do you mean?

Giselle:  I mean it's time to get away from it

Katy:  How do I do that?..I work with him

Martine:  Go on a vacation

Katy:  I hear you guys..But..I think that I will do it my way..I will be very careful and try to keep Jim out of it

Giselle:  What about your love for Jim?

Katy:  What about it?..I still love my husband

Martine:  How could you love that guy and love your husband at the same time

Katy:  Easy..By just being human..And not being fake..Where do you guys get the rule that you can't love two people at the same time?

Giselle:  We found the rule in a book called..Don't be a cheater

Martine:  In the other book called being a married woman

Katy:  Shut up guys..This is not funny

Giselle:  I am not trying to be funny

Katy:  Giselle..How many children you have?

Giselle:  Why you are asking me?..I was playing babe..You are offended?..If you want to know..I have two children..And they are both from the same man

Katy: I am not insinuating that you are a cheater..You didn't have to say from the same man..My question to you is..You love both children..Right?

Martine: Yes

Katy: Ok then..You can definitely love two people at the same time

Giselle: That is different from loving two men

Katy: How so?..Love is love..Let say that society had a rule against loving both children..Then you would have seen a problem in loving both children..It's all about what society makes you believe

Giselle: Whatever Katy..I think you are crazy..You better be careful..Once Jim found out about that..I don't want to hear it..Don't call me

Katy: What kind of friend is that?

Martine: Think about it..If my husband finds out that you are messing around with that guy..That could jeopardize my marriage as well

Katy: Whatever guys..I love you..I hear what you have to say..But I think I am going to do me..If you were in my position..You would have done the same thing

Martine: What is that position?

Katy: If you were working with a fine nice and sexy guy you would have done the same thing

Martine: Whatever Katy

Giselle: Hopefully it's just a phase..A small chapter and it will be over soon

Martine: A very dangerous chapter..I love you Katy..Let me know if you need anything..You are so crazy

Katy: I guess we need some crazy ones to have a complete world..Guys look at the time..I got to go..My massage is scheduled at six

Giselle: Can they squeeze me in?

Katy: Sure they can..They have so many good looking guys there

Martine: I am not looking for that..I am happily married

Katy: Whatever Martine..I am happily married too

Giselle: I think you are too happily married

Katy: I was about to tell you guys about my plan..But I don't think you are ready for it

Giselle: What is it?..You are moving in with him?

Katy: That's close..He is moving in with me..Jim left for Europe this morning..I want Alex to come and spend a couple days with me

Giselle: That right there..I did not hear it

Martine: Me either..Do you really know who you are married to..Do you know what he can do to you

Giselle: I thought you were crazy before..I think you are beyond crazy

Katy: Call it what you want..Are you guys coming with me?..Come..I will pay for your session

Giselle: Free massage..Great..Let's go Martine..Mrs. happy is really happy

Katy: This is a gift to you guys..So..You can stay out of my business

Giselle: You did not have to do that..That business is too hot for me

Martine: Tell me about it..It's the same as stealing from the IRS

Katy: Really?..You guys like to exaggerate


_The next day at the office


Katy: How are you Alex

Alex: I am fine..Did not sleep too well last night

Katy: What's wrong..You will sleep better tonight

Alex: Why is that?

Katy: Because my bed is very comfortable

Alex: He left?

Katy: Yes..He did..That means..You are coming home with me

Alex: Are you sure that the coast is clear?

Katy: What do you mean?

Alex: You sure Jim did not leave any snitch to watch over you while he is gone?

Katy: Why would you think so..He is not that way at all

Alex: I think you are naïve..It would not be such a big thing for a guy who put a GPS in your car to do

Katy: I told you the GPS thing was for fun..Are you coming or not..I have everything ready for us to have fun..I went on a shopping spree just for that

Alex: Shopping spree?

Katy: You will see when you come by..Are you coming?

Alex: I can still sign off

Katy: No..It's too late..You are in..You are coming home with me..You can't bring your car to my house

Alex: It's a decent car..It's fairly new

Katy: This is not what I mean

Alex: You mean Honda is not allowed on your property

Katy: Not at all..Don't put word in my mouth..My very first car was a Honda..They make great cars..You just can't bring another car to my yard..It will attract attention..So..You will drop your car home and I will pick you up

Alex: Deal..I am all the way in


_Alex and Katy are very excited about their romantic adventure..They are not aware that Jim is a step ahead of them..They have no idea that Jim had hired a private investigator to monitor their every move..That evening..Alex called his friend Frantz on the phone..Let's listen:


Frantz: What's going on?..You did not work today..I passed by your job and I did not see your car

Alex: I was at work..I had dropped my car at home

Frantz: You dropped it home?

Alex: I was riding with Katy..Actually..I am at her house right now

Frantz: Which house?..Jim's house?.. Congratulations

Alex: I know you are being sarcastic..But..Thanks anyway

Frantz: What are you doing inside the man's home Alex?

Alex: I am not an intruder..I was invited in..You have to remember this is not just Jim's home..That's Kate's home as well

Frantz: Who is Kate?

Alex:  Katy..That's her nickname

Frantz:  Ok..You have a nickname for her too

Alex:  She loves it when I call her Kate

Frantz:  You know what rhyme with Kate

Alex:  What?

Frantz:  Bate

Alex:  I am having a good time brother..You worry too much..Katy and I..We think the same way

Frantz:  Ok..Good for you..But..One thing I want you to remember..When things get ugly..Do not get me involved..You hear me

Katy:  Who are you talking too?..I want you all for myself

Alex:  That's Frantz..You want to say hello to him?

Frantz:  Dude..What's a matter with you..I don't want to talk

Alex:  Here

Katy:  Hello Frantz

Frantz:  Hi..How are you?

Katy:  I am great..I want you to know that your friend is here with me..He is in good hands..I will take good care of him

Frantz:  Great..Have fun

Katy:  We sure will..Talk to you later..Let me put your buddy back on the phone

Frantz:  Take care

Alex:  She sounds happy..Doesn't she?..She is in love

Frantz:  Bro..I told you not to get me involved in your shenanigans

Alex:  You heard what she said..I am in good hands..She will take good care of me

Frantz:  Exactly..Tell her to cremate your body once Jim is done with you

Katy:  You like the red one?

Alex:  That's nice..I like the pink one better

Frantz: What pink one?..Are you losing your mind?

Alex: Not you dude..I was talking to Katy..She is trying on some under garments for me

Frantz: Ok playboy..Do your things..I have things to do around here..Talk to you later

Alex: I will keep you informed

Frantz: Informed about what?

Alex: About my romantic adventure

Frantz: Dude..You just don't get it..You are messing around with Jim Castillo's wife..Inside his house..You call that a romantic adventure?..That sounds more like a death wish adventure to me

Alex: C'mon..Don't be so negative

Frantz: I am negative..I am telling it the way it is..Later dude

Katy: Babe..The bath is ready..Are you coming or not?

Frantz: She is calling you

Alex: Yep..Guess what she is calling me for?

Frantz: I don't care

Alex: For a bath..This is heaven bro

Frantz: Yep..There will be another bath once Jim finds out

Alex: What bath is that?

Frantz: A blood bath

Alex: You don't understand Frantz..This is heaven

Frantz: I know..Once Jim finds out..There will be heaven as well..This time it will be a one way trip

Alex: Peace brother..You are just hating

Frantz: Later


_Later that day..Tony gets a call


Jim: Tony..How are you?

Tony:  I am ok..I thought you were in Europe..You did not go?

Jim:  Yes..I went..I am there now..What's a matter?..There is no phone in Europe?

Tony:  I never said that..The guy who invented the phone was from Europe..Wasn't he?

Jim:  No..He is American..Wasn't it Alexander Bell who invented the phone?

Tony:  I don't know all that..I only use that thing..I don't know who invented it..By the way I would like to see him to have a word or two with him

Jim:  About what?

Tony:  My phone does not keep charge at all

Jim:  C'mon Tony..You can't blame the guy for your cell phone..The phone he invented was the size of a Volkswagen

Tony:  Tell me about it..Why are you calling..Aren't you supposed to be enjoying your vacation?

Jim:  I know..I just want you to check on that guy for me

Tony:  What guy?

Jim:  The investigator..Make sure he is doing the job ok..I left him a key so he could install some cameras in the house for me..I want you to get the key from him once he is done..I don't want him to have the key to my house for too long..He could be the fed

Tony:  The kid is not the fed..You are paranoid Jim..Don't worry about that..Enjoy your vacation..Stop spying on my girl Katy..She is innocent

Jim:  I don't know about that Tony..My gut feelings tells me different

Tony:  Well your gut is wrong this time..You need to take a laxative or something..By the way how are your old folks?..Are they ok?

Jim:  I spoke to them on the phone..I am still in France..I haven't seen them yet..I will be in Italy Thursday

Tony:  Have fun..Stop being paranoid..You know if my girl knows you are doing that you will be history

Jim:  I know..I know..Say hello to all the guys for me..Did you guys play?

Tony:  No..You know there is no poker game when you are not there

Jim:  Really?..My money is that good?

Tony:  We love it

Jim:  I see..See you later brother..I have to catch a train here..Get the key from that crook for me

Tony:  Don't worry..I got you.. Talk to you later brother..Have some fun..Get some real French toasts and good wines and cheese

Jim:  Also some real French fries..Not the bootleg ones we have in America

Tony:  This is the only case where the bootleg is better than the original

Jim:  Tell me about it..Later


_Later at Jim's house..Katy and Alex go into the pool


Katy:  It feels so good to be here with you..Alone..And wearing our birth outfits

Alex:  It is so warm?

Katy:  It is heated..So deep..Ugh

Alex:  The pool?

Katy:  Never mind..I never thought I would be able to have so much fun..I thought my life was over after I got married

Alex:  But you said that you love your husband

Katy:  I do..But..With you it's totally different..It's a different feeling

Alex:  You meant the pool does not feel so deep and warm when you are with Jim in it?

Katy:  Very funny..Don't you make fun of my husband

Alex:  Why are we whispering?

Katy:  You never know..People are nosy

Alex:  I thought you said the nearest neighbor is three football fields away

Katy:  Yes..But at night sound travels better and further

Alex:  You are so right

Katy:  Let's go inside

Alex:  Ok

_Alex and Katy are having a great time..It is like a honeymoon vacation..Katy takes two weeks off from work and orders Alex to take vacation as well..They are really having a great time..But..Time flies..The fun is soon over..Jim is home from Europe..Let's listen:

Jim: Hello..Hello darling..How are you..You look so tan

Katy: I know..This is not a tan..This is really dark

Jim: You went to the beach?

Katy: No not at all..I spent a lot of time by the pool

Jim: Great..This is why I have it here..It's for you to have fun..I am glad you are making good use of it

Katy: The one on the top floor was my idea

Jim: I know..I will give you credit for that..Everybody is asking for you

Katy: How is everybody?

Jim: They are fine..They wanted to give me so many things to bring for you

Katy: I know you..You don't like to carry stuffs

Jim: Not at all..If I was travelling private..It would be a different story

Katy: I don't know why you did not go private?

Jim: No..I didn't want to be in a whole plane by myself for such a long time..I wanted to see people..By the way I made a new friend

Katy: A woman?

Jim: Some French guy..His name is Francois

Katy: Aren't they all Francois?

Jim: It seems so..But..He is a very nice guy..What's on your neck..It's all red

Katy: It must be mosquito bites

Jim: All your shoulders are red

Katy: I know..I also have sun burns.. What do you want me to do..Should I ask the lady to prepare a bath for you?

Jim: No..I will just take a shower and get some sleep..The jetlag is killing me

Katy:  What do you want to eat?

Jim:  Your phone is ringing

Katy:  Hello..Alex..How are you..How was work today?..You missec me during those days..This is Alex..The guy at work

Jim:  Ok..Say hello to him for me..Is he behaving?

Katy:  Jim asked me if you are behaving..What should I say?

Alex:  Yes..Of course


_The next day..Jim met with the private investigator


Jim:  Hello

PI:  Hello..Mr. Castillo..How are you sir?

Jim:  I am fine..Do you have anything for me?

PI:  Yes sir..I have some stuff for you

Jim:  Good stuffs?..Don't  waste my time?

PI:  I promise..I am not going to waste your time

Jim:  Ok..Why don't you meet me at the parking lot of the McDonald

PI:  Which one sir?

Jim:  The one at Orchard Street

PI:  No problem..I will be there in five minutes


_A few minutes later Jim arrives at the meeting place


Jim:  Hello..Where are you?

PI:  I am here

Jim:  Come to my car..The black Cadillac

PI: I see you

Jim: Hi..How are you kid?

PI: I am fine

Jim: What do you have for me?..Did you see her with any guy?

PI: Yes I did..This is the first video..This guy is getting in her car at work and they drove off

Jim: This is the kid who works with her..I know that guy..Not that I know him..I met him before

PI: Well..It gets better..In this feed right here..This one is from the cameras we installed at your house..That's him walking in your bedroom shirtless

Jim: Who is that in the room

PI: That's your wife sir..She seems to be doing some modeling for him

Jim: Really?..Are you sure this is not made up..You know if you make up stuff about my wife you are dead..Right?

PI: Why would I do such thing sir?..I am a very professional guy..Everything you see there is legit..Shall I continue..If you see enough let me know please

Jim: Go ahead..Play the video

PI: They left the room and went in the pool..Right here..You can see they are getting really romantic in the pool

Jim: Really?..They are having sex in my pool..If this is true?..That guy is dead

PI: Well sir..Our intent is not to get people hurt or kill

Jim: Listen..You know who I am..Don't you?

PI: No sir

Jim: Give me the video..I need to talk to her about this

PI: Here they are sir

Jim: How much I have for you?

PI: For the work and materials used..It will be two thousands and five hundreds

Jim: Three thousands in this stock here..Listen to me..Nobody should know about this..If I find out that people talking about my wife..About those videos at all..You are dead..You hear me..I did not hear your answer..You are dead..Do you understand me?

PI: Yes sir

Jim: Now..Get off my damn car..I am sorry..I am pissed off..Not at you

PI: I understand


_ Jim puts his Cadillac on drive and leaves tire marks at the McDonald parking lot and into the streets..He reaches home in no time..Katy is on the phone with one of her girl friends and unaware of what is coming her way..

-Ok..Guys..My loving readers..I know it's getting crazy..But..We cannot miss this one..Let's sneak in inside Jim's house and listen:


Jim: KATY..KATY..WHERE ARE YOU ?..KATY..KATY..WHERE ARE YOU?

Katy: I am here

Chantal: That's Jim screaming your name like that?

Katy: He must have lost his mind..Let me see what he needs Chantal..I will call you later

Jim: WHERE ARE YOU?

Katy: Jim..What is a matter with you?..Have you lost your mind..What is the reason you are screaming my name like a wild animal?

Jim: I think you are in fact the wild animal

Katy: Jim..Don't be disrespectful..You never behaved like that towards me..What is a matter with you?

Jim: I need you to see something

Katy: What is it?

Jim: Come in the room with me

Katy: What all this is about?..What's wrong with you?

Jim: Watch this..Who is this getting in the car with you?

Katy: That's Alex..You met Alex..Did you not?..This is why you are acting like an animal?

Jim: Wait..It gets better

Katy: You are wasting my time

Jim: I am not..Who is this in my bedroom..Shirtless..Who is this modeling underwear?..Who?

Katy: That's what you are doing now? Spying on me?

Jim: Spying?..This is my house..Who are those people in my house Katy..Answer me?

Katy: I have nothing to say to you

Jim: Don't you walk away from me when I am talking to you

Katy: Jim..Let go of my arm..You are hurting me..Let go of me

Jim: Where are you going?

Katy: What did you do..You threw the glass and broke my mirror

Jim: It will soon be your face if you don't give me an answer

Katy: Move out of the way Jim..I need to get out of this room

Jim: No you are not

Katy: Yes I am too..Let go of my shirt..You tore my shirt..I will call the police for you Jim

Jim: Go ahead call the police..You will be dead before they get here..Don't you run from me..Get out of the damn closet..Get out now

Katy: No..I am not..I am calling my friends

Jim: Get out

Chantal: Hello..Katy..Are you ok?

Katy: No..Jim is acting crazy..He is breaking up stuffs all over the house

Chantal: What is a matter?

Katy: I will tell you later

Chantal: You want me to have Tony call him

Katy: Yes..I am so afraid

Chantal: Where are you?

Katy: I am in my closet..I locked the door..I can hear him breaking up stuffs in the room..Tell Tony to call him..Please

Chantal: Ok..I will tell my husband to call him..Stay in there

Katy: Hurry up

Jim: Hello..This is not a good time Tony..Bye..Get out of the closet or I will shoot down the door

Katy: Jim..Calm down..Or.. I will call the police

Jim: Let me see you bring the police to my house..I want to see that

Katy: Stop

Tony: Hello

Jim: Tony..I told you that I can't talk now

Tony: You are not going to hang up the phone again Jim..What is a matter..Chantal told me you are going crazy over there

Jim: Tony..You would not believe what I saw Katy doing on a video

Tony: What video?

Jim: The video I got from the PI

Tony: Listen..Tony..I don't care what is on the video..This is not the way we handle business..What are you going to do?..Hurt her..Then she calls the police..You want the police to get involved?..Calm down..Talk to Katy..Ask her why she did what she did..There is always a reason behind an action..That was not an accident..Therefore..She must have a reason for doing it..This is your wife..You guys have been together forever..Talk to her..Where is she?

Jim: She is hiding in the closet

Tony: By the way who is the guy on the video?

Jim: The guy she works with

Tony: I thought that kid was smarter than that..Well..We are going to deal with it accordingly..But..You can't act up and get the police involved..You hear me..Calm down..I heard you are breaking everything in the house

Jim: I broke a couple stuffs

Tony: Those are expensive stuffs..Why are breaking them

Jim: I was pissed off..I cut my finger too when I punched the mirror..I am still pissed off..But I calm down a little

Tony: Talk to her and find out why she is doing it..I don't think she does not love you..But..There is a reason..Find out the reason..And leave the rest of the job for the guys to handle..You know we don't play

Jim: No problem..Let me handle it

Tony: Ok


_Meanwhile


Robert: Alex..Your phone is ringing

Alex: Hello..Hello..I can barely hear you..What's a matter?

Katy: It's me..Katy

Alex: I know..Are you ok?

Katy: No..Jim is going crazy here

Alex: What happened?

Katy: He found out that you were here at the house

Alex: What?..Did you say he found out that I was at your place?

Katy: Yes

Alex: Oh my god..Are you serious?

Katy: Yes

Alex: Where are you?

Katy: I am in my closet..I locked the door..He is breaking everything

Alex: Are you going to be ok..You want me to come?

Katy: To come where?..You want to die?..I think you should leave town

Alex: Leaving town?..You are crazy..He does not know what I look like..He only saw me once..I can always say that I was there to bring you some documents from work

Katy: No..He has a video

Alex: I am in the video?..What is in the video?

Katy: Everything

Alex: I did not hear what you say?..You are talking too low

Katy: I said..Everything is on the video..Everything we did

Alex: This is more serious than I thought

Katy: It is very serious..You can no longer come near me ok

Alex: What about my job?

Katy: No..We can no longer work together..Jim will kill you if he sees you..I have to go..He is calling me

Alex: Are you going to be ok?

Katy: I will be fine..Worry about yourself..I think he calms down..Tony called him on the phone..Leave town if you can

Alex: You can forget that..I am not leaving town..I am not afraid of him..He is a man and I am a man..Let him bring it

Katy: I have to go

Alex: Bye

Robert: What's going on?

Alex: I need a gun..I need a gun Robert..I need a gun right now

Robert: What are you talking about?

Alex: You hear what I said

Robert: You need a gun?..For what?

Alex: Jim found out that I was at his house

Robert: So..What is the big deal?..You had to bring some work materials to her

Alex: He had us on video

Robert: What?..You do need a gun..Wow..This is serious

Alex: She said if Jim sees me he will kill me..I can no longer work with her

Robert: This is crazy..Call Frantz

Frantz: Hello

Alex: Frantz..You were right

Frantz: About what?

Alex: You were right..He found out..He found out

Frantz: What are you talking about?

Alex: Jim

Frantz: Jim who?

Alex: Jim Castillo

Frantz: What about him?

Alex: He found out that Katy and I were messing around

Frantz: Alex..Why are you telling me this?..Didn't I tell you when things get ugly I don't want to know about it

Alex: Listen man..I think we need a gun

Frantz: Did you say we?

Alex: Well..You are involved too

Frantz: Involved how?

Alex: Where can I get a gun?

Frantz: Are you asking me? You must be crazy..You remember what I told you Alex..You don't want to listen..This time my dude..You are on your own..I am not going to lose my life for nonsense

Alex: It's too late for blames Frantz..What do you think I should do?

Frantz: Why don't you ask your partner in crime..Katy?

Alex: Katy thinks I should leave town completely

Frantz: Dude..I really don't know..I am not involved in this mess..I am right now shopping for flowers to send to Nancy..Trying to prevent her from leaving me..I have enough to deal with

Alex: This is crazy

Frantz: How did he find out anyway?

Alex: He had a video surveillance at his home..Dude..He saw everything

Frantz: What do you mean?

Alex: He saw me getting it in

Frantz: You are so dead brother..I just feel sorry for your mom and dac

Alex: Dude..Stop playing already..All jokes aside..It's whatever..You know me Frantz..I am not afraid of any man

Frantz: Good luck warrior..This is not my war..I will watch it on the news

Alex: Seriously Frantz..Do you think I should get a gun?

Frantz: I think you should get a nuclear weapon arsenal

Alex: You play too much

Frantz: All of the sudden you want to get serious now..I thought you were having fun?..What happened to the fun part?

Alex: Talk to you later..I will handle it..I am not a punk..You already know

Frantz: Good to hear..Handle it without calling my phone..I will apprec ate it if you could do just that


_Meanwhile At the Castillo's home


Jim: Come out already..I need to talk to you

Katy: I will come out Jim..If you put your hand on me or threat me..I will call the police

Jim: Come out..No one will put hand on you..I need to talk to you..This is very serious..We need to talk

Katy: Oh my god Jim..What have you done to my room?

Jim: I had to release the anger somewhere..Have a seat..Tell me..What is this about..You could have told me that you don't love me anymore..But you did not have to cheat on me

Katy: I never said I didn't love you Jim..I love you..You are my husband

Jim: You love me?..The video said something totally different

Katy: Not at all..I just wanted to have fun

Jim: That's your idea of having fun

Katy: Well..It is..I like to be free..I want to do what I want..What will make me feel good..This is what I wanted to do..I wanted to experience having a romantic relation with him..So..I did that

Jim: Do you know what being married means?

Katy: Yes I do

Jim: Do you know what being married to Jim Castillo means?

Katy: What do you mean?

Jim: That means..This is a very important decision..Any disrespect to the family is punishable by death..You know that right

Katy: I don't know what you are talking about Jim..I did not do anything to you personally..You were not involved..It was just me and Alex..How did I do something to you?..Explain it to me..This is my body..I share it to whomever I please

Jim: This is the way you see it..Ok..For your information..We will deal with it accordingly

Katy: Jim..I don't know what you mean..Alex should not pay for that..I was the one who dragged him into it

Jim: I don't care about what you are saying there..He knows you are my wife..He knows this is my house..He violated me and disrespected all my guys..God bless his soul

Katy: Jim..Are you done talking?

Jim: You are in a rush to go meet him

Katy: Not that at all..I see you are getting angry again..I want to get away from that

Jim: You are to stay inside the house and don't put your feet out

Katy: What are you saying?..I am not a prisoner

Jim: I am trying to protect your life..The guys might take actions against you for the disrespect

Katy: Jim..I am not going to live my life in fear..This is my life..This is my body..I do what I want with it..Tell your guys to get lost

Jim: We will deal with it fast and efficiently

Katy: Can I get away now?

Jim: Whatever..Get out of my face


_Phone is ringing


Tony: Hello..Jim..What's going on?..You calmed down..You sound better

Jim: I need a meeting with all the guys tonight

Tony: Certainly..We need to act fast before he leaves town

Jim: Tony..I need all the guys here..All of them

Tony: I hear you..At what time?

Jim: Nine o'clock

Tony: Ok boss..What do we do with her?

Jim: I haven't decided yet..Meanwhile..She is to stay in the bedroom and don't go anywhere

Tony: Will let them know


_A week later..Katy called Alex on the phone


Katy: Hello

Alex: Hey stranger..What are you doing calling my phone?

Katy: I am calling you to give you a heads up regarding the whole situation

Alex: Everything cooled off

Katy: No..They are about to come after you

Alex: Come after me?..You are kidding

Katy: I am not kidding..They had a meeting about it

Alex: Really?

Katy: Really..I am so afraid for you..They had a major meeting..All his guys were here at the house

Alex: Ok..Ok..It's all good

Katy: It's not all good..You need to get out of town

Alex: Not going to happen..I am not leaving ..I am from here..My family is here..My mom..My dad is here

Katy: I thought you said that your dad passed away?

Alex: My step dad..I called him dad..You tell Jim I am not going anywhere

Katy:  you are so naïve Alex

Alex:  Katy..Katy..Stop..I am a man baby..You think I am going to run from another man..Everybody has to die someday..One thing I know for sure..If it's not my day to go..Someone else will get it..I did not know when I was born..So.. I don't worry at all about the time I am leaving

Katy:  Anyway..Just be careful..I know Jim and his crew don't play

Alex:  Me and my crew we don't play either

Katy:  Who is in your crew?

Alex:  Frantz..Myself and a couple of guys

Katy:  Your friend Frantz?

Alex:  I know right..He would kill me if he hears me

Katy:  I am not allowed to go anywhere

Alex:  You want me to come and rescue you?

Katy:  Stop playing Alex..I have to go

Alex:  One question..Do you miss me?

Katy:  Bye Alex..You play too much

Alex:  Bye


Robert:  What is happening?

Alex:  I am a wanted man..You might think it's crazy..I feel good about it though

Robert:  Alex..You are crazy..This is a serious situation

Alex:  I am a little crazy..You know one thing..I always dream of a society without rules

Robert:  Really?..For what though?

Alex:  Just to see how much damage I would do..Just the old west type of society..The purge type of society

Robert:  That movie the purge was crazy.. You are crazy my dude

Alex: I am kidding..But..On a serious note though..I really don't worry that much about Jim..I know.. I should not have had a romantic relation with his wife..But it's already done..It's not just me..She wanted that

Robert: I think you need to take some serious measures..Change your way about

Alex: Who is talking? Frantz or Robert?


_Later that day..Frantz is getting home from doing some shopping for his girlfriend Nancy..He pulls up to his parking lot and two cars pull nearby..Four guys get out with gun in hands..Let's listen:


Jim's guy: Don't do anything stupid..Get in the damn car

Frantz: Watch out with the gun dude

Jim's guy: You watch out..Get in the car right now

Frantz: What is this about?

Jim's guy: We ask the questions..And pay attention..We are not going to repeat the questions twice

Frantz: What is this about..What is that about..Don't push me dude

Jim's guy: Listen up..You know the boss' wife?

Frantz: I don't know what you are talking about

Jim's guy: Do you know Katy?

Frantz: I don't know any Katy

Jim's guy: We can do this the nice way or a little different..One more time..The boss GPS revealed that she was here at your place..Now..Are you going to tell the true or not?..Claudio..Drive the car

Frantz: Katy..Katy..I remember her..She stopped by for a few minutes to see a friend

Jim's guy: Exactly..This is what we are talking about..Alex is your friend name..Right?

Frantz: Yes

Jim's guy: He is your friend right?

Frantz: Yes

Jim's guy: This is where it gets very serious..The boss wants him alive..To talk to him before he can decide his fate..He needs you to help us capture your friend alive..It's up to you..You can refuse and your girlfriend will die..You know that person?..Look at this picture

Frantz: That's my girlfriend Nancy..Where did you get her picture?

Jim's guy: Remember..You don't ask questions..We ask the questions here..You help us bring your friend in..And your girlfriend and you will be safe..Otherwise..Both of you will be dead soon

Frantz: Dead?..What are you talking about?..I did not do anything

Jim's guy: Yes you did..You provided your friend with a place to meet with the boos' wife

Frantz: I did not provide anything to anyone

Jim's guy: Listen carefully..If you go to the police you and your girlfriend are dead..If you tell your friend about our plan..You are also dead..You understand?

Frantz: Whatever dude

Jim's guy: I need a yes or no..Do you understand?

Frantz: I said whatever

Jim's guy: Blow up his knee

Frantz: No..Don't shoot..Don't shoot

Jim's guy: Do you understand?

Frantz: Yes..Yes

Jim's guy: Now..What is your phone number?..We will contact you to tell you what we need you to do..Let him out guys


_Meanwhile


Katy: Hello Giselle

Giselle: Katy..Are you ok?..We are not allowed to talk to you

Katy: C'mon Giselle..You are going to listen to those guys..We are friends

Giselle: My husband is already accusing me of knowing and helping you do what you did..It's best we stop talking for a while..Wait until their heads cool off

Katy: I will call Martine

Giselle:  She is not allowed to talk to you either

Katy:  Ok..I need some feminine stuff..I can't stay locked up in a room

Giselle:  Be careful..His guys may do stuffs to you

Katy:  I am going out anyway

Giselle:  Be careful Katy..They are really angry

Katy:  Talk to you later

Giselle:  Don't go t the pharmacy that is right around the corner

Katy:  I know..I will go to the one in the next town

Giselle:  Bye..Take care..If you don't hear from me Katy..You know why

Katy:  No problem..I have no friends now..I get it..Bye


_Since Jim was not home..After she hangs up the phone..Katy gets in her car and drives to the pharmacy..It was getting a little dark already..Ten minutes later a white van just pushes Katy car's into the right shoulder ditch..Luckily she is not injured..She cannot get the car out..She does not want to call the police..Most of all she does not want to let her husband know she is out driving..She tries calling Giselle but she does not answer her phone..She calls Martine but she does not answer the phone either..Her mind is racing..She feels all alone in a bad situation..She does a dangerous thing..She calls Alex..Alex answers the phone..Let's listen:


Alex:  Hello..Who is this?

Katy:  What do you mean who is this?..It's me Alex..You don't know my number..You forget my voice already..It's me Katy

Alex:  I saw it was your number..But..I was not sure who was calling..It could have been Jim using your phone..What are doing calling me anyway Katy?

Katy:  I am in trouble

Alex:  What's wrong?

Katy:  I've been locked up in the house for too long..So..I needed some stuff..I was driving to the pharmacy then a van pushed my car into the ditch

Alex: Really?..And where is the driver of the van?

Katy: He did not stop

Alex: He did not stop?..You think it could be Jim's guys?

Katy: No doubt about it

Alex: You are so brave Katy..You are so calm about it

Katy: What should I do?..Kill myself..I am not afraid of them..Jim will not harm me..He probably wants his guys to intimidate me..But..You are the one in danger..They will kill you Alex

Alex: You think so

Katy: I know so

Alex: Where are you?

Katy: I am in the road between Mongo town and Louisville's township

Alex: That road is completely dark..I am on my way

Katy: No..No Alex..Don't come


_Alex gets into his car and drives towards Katy..In no time he is there


Katy: Alex..Alex..You came..You are going to get both of us killed..You are so brave..I thought you were a chicken

Alex: What am I supposed to do?..You are stuck on the road..None of your friends want to help you..So..I am here

Katy: That's so brave of you

Alex: I don't let fear govern my life..Too often someone who needs help approaches us and because of our fear we turn him or her away..Someone can be in a real difficult situation..Stranded somewhere..That person could reach out to us for help and we turn our backs on him or her due to fear..I refuse to let fear overshadow my compassion for others

Katy: Alex..This situation is more dangerous..If they find you with me we will be both dead

Alex: Even though I have to put my life in danger by being here with you..I could not just ignore you..Your friends are too afraid to come to your assistance..What kind of friends are they?

Katy: It's ok..My brave Alex is here..That's what count

Alex: Let me call a tow truck for you

Katy: Thanks..I can drive it back home

Alex: Sure..I don't see much damage..Just a tiny mark on the back bumper where the van hit you..Come sit in my car..The tow truck guy said he will be here in seven minutes..Come sit in my car..It's pretty cold out there

Katy: Thanks Alex..You are an angel

Alex: I know..Your husband is trying to make a real one out of me

Katy: No one contacted you yet

Alex: What do you mean?

Katy: Jim's guy didn't contact you yet?

Alex: Contact me?..I don't play Katy..I play with women only..I don't play with guys..I am prepared to fight back

Katy: You are so brave..You become insane

Alex: I learn to be brave from my dog..When I was little I had a dog..My friends will bring their dogs around to fight my dog..My dog never backed down..He always put out a good fight..It's like he did not want to disappoint me..He fought every one of them..So..From that time I learn to be brave..You don't go out and look for the fight..But..If the fight comes your way and you can't avoid it..You put up your best fight

Katy: Ok..Ok..Strange way to learn about bravery..My dogs did not teach me anything..Maybe licking faces

Alex: Very funny..The guys are here..The tow truck

Katy: Go talk to them..I don't want them to see me..They might know Jim..He knows all the mechanics around town

Alex: Don't worry..I will talk to them

Tow Guy: That's a nice ride you have there

Alex: Yeah..How much will it be?

Tow Guy: It's going to be two fifty to pull it out..The ditch is not too deep

Alex: Alright

Tow Guy:  Whose car is it?..Yours?

Alex:  No..My friend's car..Try not to damage it

Tow Guy:  Of course not..That's expensive right there baby


_ In fifteen minutes the car is out of the ditch


Katy:  What should I do?..Should I go back home or proceed to the pharmacy?

 Alex:  If you really need the stuffs you were going to get..Go get them..I will follow you there

Katy:  Thank you so much


_Fifteen  minutes later


Alex:  That was pretty fast

Katy:  I just needed a couple things

Alex:  What were they?

Katy:  You are too nosy Alex..Ladies' stuff..I could have sent one of the ladies who work there to go get it for me..I just wanted to be outside for a moment

Alex:  Your hands are cold..Come in my car for a minute

Katy:  Alex..This is not a good idea..I have to get going..I can't believe I am sitting in your car..This is so crazy

Alex:  Let me pull into the back parking lot

Katy:  I haven't been outside for so  many days

Alex:  It's pretty dark out right there..No one can see us

Katy:  Your hand is so warm..It  feels so good

Alex:  Your body is warm as well..I miss you so much

Katy:  I miss you too

Alex: It feels so good..Keep going


_A couple of days later


Jim's guys: Hello

Frantz: Hello

Jim's guy: We want you to help us get a key to his apartment

Frantz: Whose apartment?

Jim's guy: Your friend's apartment..Whatever his name is..Alex

Frantz: What for?

Jim's guy: You don't ask questions

Frantz: I have a key to his place

Jim's guy: We will pick it up from you in ten minutes..We are going to need it tonight


_ Jim's friends come to Frantz's place and pick up the key..After they leave his place..Frantz races to a locksmith store and purchases a new door lock and makes his way to Alex's place


Alex: What are you doing here?..You did not tell me you were coming by

Frantz: I need a screw driver..Hurry up

Alex: Hold your horse partner..Something is wrong with your car?

Frantz: Give me the screwdriver

Alex: What are you doing?

Frantz: I need to change your door knob

Alex: What?..Are you crazy?..For what?

Frantz: Yes..I need to do that now

Alex: Frantz ..You are losing your mind..Dude you removed my door knob?..What's a matter with you

Frantz: I am replacing it by this one

Alex: What happened..You had a bad dream..Dude..This is insane..You need to go see a doctor

Frantz: I am trying to prevent you from seeing one

Alex: You think it is normal behavior..You came here..Grabbed a screwdriver and changed my door knob

Frantz: I got to go..Here are your new keys

Alex: Dude..I need to change my toilet seat too..You don't do toilet


_Later that night..At around one in the morning..Jim's guys go to Alex's apartment..To their biggest surprise the key Frantz had given to them did not work..The next morning one of them called Frantz on the phone..Let's listen:


Frantz: Hello

Jim's guy: What did you do?

Frantz: What did I do?

Jim's guy: You gave us a wrong key

Frantz: Not at all..That's the only key I had for his place

Jim's guy: You think it's a game..Don't you?

Frantz: Check the key..Does it say the name of the apartment complex on it?

Jim's guy: Yes it does..How come it did not work?

Frantz: I have no idea..He must have changed his lock

Jim's guy: I need you to call him now..We will do a three way call..I need to know where he is now..Call him

Frantz: No problem

Alex: Hello..Frantz..What's going on?

Frantz: Where are you?

Alex: You are not going to act crazy like you did yesterday

Frantz: Alex..Shut up now and listen

Alex: What?

Frantz: Where are you?

Alex: I am at the mall with Isabelle..We are having lunch at the food ccurt..Well..Not lunch yet..Smoothies and waiting for a sandwich..You want to say hello to her..Are you coming?

Frantz: No..I am not..See you later

Alex: Why did you call me then?

Frantz: Bye

Jim's guy: We will go get him in a few

Frantz: No problem


_Frantz hangs up the phone..Jumps in his car and heads towards the mall


_Meanwhile


Alex: Frantz has been acting weird lately

Isabelle: Why would you say that?..He is always calm

Alex: Yesterday..He came to my apartment and he changed my door knob without my permission

Isabelle: What?..That's funny

Alex: You call it funny..That's crazy


_A few minutes later..Frantz arrives at the mall..Runs through the fooc court looking for his friend..And finally finds him


Alex: Dude..What are you doing here?..I thought you said you were not coming?

Frantz: let's go

Alex: Let's go where?

Frantz:  Let's go..You have to leave now

Alex:  Frantz..Stop acting crazy my brother..Have a seat..You did not say hello to Isabelle

Frantz:  Dude..Let's go

Alex:  Let's go where?..I am eating my sandwich

Frantz:  Now you are done eating..Let's go

Alex:  You threw my sandwich in the trash..How rude is that?..You know you are going to give me my money back..You how much the sandwich cost?

Frantz:  I am sorry Isabelle

Isabelle:  I am fine..It was not my food

Alex:  What is the problem?

Frantz:  You want to know..Sorry Isabelle

Alex:  Don't be pulling from my arm like that

Frantz:  Listen Alex..Jim sent his guys after you..They are on their way here to get you

Alex:  How do you know that?

Frantz:  They came after me and want me to help them to get you..See..Look over there

Alex:  Where?

Frantz:  See those two guys over there..They are here

Alex:  I saw them

Frantz:  Dude let's run into the restroom before they see us

Alex:  I think they did already


_Unfortunately for Frantz and Alex..Jim's guys saw them running into the bathroom..They made their way upstairs and into the bathroom

Ok..My loving readers..I know it's dangerous to go in there..We cannot miss the action..Let's go in


Alex:  Are you guys following us?

Jim's guy:  Yes..We are here to take you with us


_At that very moment..Alex lifts the front of his shirt and reveals the taped grip of a forty five tuck into the front of his pants..Following that..Frantz pulls a three eighty from his pants pocket and brings a round into the chamber..The hunters become the hunted..Let's listen:


Jim's guy:  Easy with the gun

Frantz:  You don't give orders..We are in charge..Don't move..Keep your hands up..Wow..Thirty eight special in your pocket

Alex:  Hey you..Mustache man..Empty your pockets..Don't do anything stupid..You understand what a forty five can do to you at closed range..No gun..He has a knife

Frantz:  They were ready..Weren't they?

Alex:  Ready..But..They did not know who they were messing with

Frantz:  I guess not

Jim's guy:  You turned on us you

Frantz:  Turned on you?..Are you crazy?..I was never with you..I wanted to make sure my girl Nancy was safe first before bringing the fight to you..You think I was going to just help you kill my friend?..Really?..Now you understand why the key could not open his apartment door

Alex:  Tell Jim..We are the wrong guys to mess with..Let me try this watch you have there

Frantz:  No Alex..Let them out

Alex:  Get out..Before I make you go back to Jim naked


_Jim's guys left the bathroom..Very thankful because it could have been worse


Alex:  Dude..I did not know you carried a gun?

Frantz:  I did not know you had one either..They served the purpose well today

Alex:  Tell me about it

Frantz:  Why were you trying to take his watch..You have so many watches

Alex: I know right..I did not need it..I just wanted him to remember me every time he checks the time..I guess we sent a strong message to Jim

Frantz: Definitely..We have to be prepared for what comes next

Alex: It does not matter to me..Its whatever


_later that day..Jim's phone rings


Jim: Hello

Jim's guy: Boss..We had a problem

Jim: What problem?

Jim's guy: We could not bring the guy in

Jim: Why not?..Are you guys getting soft?

Jim's guy: No sir..They were both strapped

Jim: What do you mean both?..It's just one guy

Jim's guy: No boss..The other guy turned on us..He is no longer helping us..He pulled out a gun on us

Jim: Really?..Where was that?

Jim's guy: At the mall sir

Jim: Listen..I want to put the operation on hold..I have to figure out a new strategy..I don't want my name to be involved in any shootout..You guys hear me..Put everything on hold..Do not approach those guys..I did not know they had balls?

Jim's guy: Big one too..They are not punks sir..He even tried to take my watch

Jim: Really?..Ok..Everything on hold until further notice


_That night at Frantz's house


Alex: Robert..Pass me the Ciroc

Robert: We are well equipped tonight..Check this out

Alex:  You have a black bottle

Frantz:  And an Effen vodka as well

Jeff:  Who made the Effen?

Robert:  That's Fifty Cents vodka

Jeff:  I know the Ciroc is Diddy's and the Black bottle is Rozzay

Alex:  This is how you celebrate

Jeff:  What is the occasion anyway?

Mark:  Today they had an encounter with Jim's guys

Alex:  Yep..We punked them..My phone is ringing

Katy:  Hello

Alex:  Hello..Katy..How are you darling..You want to meet me in the parking lot again?

Katy:  Stop playing Alex..I called you to tell you something big is happening..Jim called for a major meeting again

Alex:  We already know that

Katy:  What do you mean?

Alex:  Jim sent his guys after us in the mall..And we punked them..They did not know we were strapped

Katy:  What do you mean strapped?

Alex:  We were armed

Katy:  You and who else?

Alex:  And Frantz

Katy:  Frantz does not look like somebody who would carry a gun

Alex:  You are wrong..He brought one into the chamber and put those guys on ice

Katy:  Really?..You guys should get ready..He is planning something major

Alex:  At this point it's whatever  Katy

Katy:  Just be careful

_That night at Jim Castillo's home


Jim: Listen up..I want to get this guy..I want to get him now

Tony: Jim..You are a business man..You don't want your name to be involved in shootout..You can't take it to the streets

Johnny: Tony is right..We have to be more tactical about it

Jim: Ok..What do you suggest Johnny

Johnny: I say we bring on charges

Jim: What are you talking about Johnny?

Johnny: You have his picture walking inside your home..Right?

Jim: Yes we do

Johnny: Get some video clips..And accuse him of rape

Jim: That's kind of dirty..Don't you think?

Tony: He is dirtier..He came inside your home and had sex with your wife..You can't have mercy for him

Jim: What do you guys say?..Everybody agrees?..What about Katy?..She can just deny it

Johnny: No..We will have a doctor to sedate her for a while..She won't be available to give any statement


_Three weeks later while the guys were at Frantz's house..Two detectives knock on the door


Frantz: Guys..Answer the door for me..I am on the phone with Nancy

Robert: No problem

Detective: Good evening..My name is detective Edwards and this is my partner Guzman

Robert: How can we help you guys?

Detective Edwards: We are looking for Alex Smith

Robert: What for?

Detective Edwards:  Is he here or not?

Frantz:  Rob..Who is it?

Robert:  Some Detectives is asking for Alex

Frantz:  For Alex?..For what?..Babe..Let me call you later..How I can I help you guys?

Detective Guzman:  We are looking for Alex Smith..Is he here?

Frantz:  Yes he is..He is in the bathroom..Alex..Alex..Some dudes are asking for you here

Alex:  Some dudes..For me?..For what?..How can I help you?

Detective Edwards:  You are under arrest sir

Alex:  Under arrest for what?

Detective:  The charge is rape sir..First degree rape

Alex:  You must be kidding..Rape who?

Frantz:  Guys..I am asking you to leave my place..My friend did not rape anybody

Detective:  Sir..We are serving a warrant

Frantz:  Where is the warrant?

Detective:  Right here..You are happy now

Frantz:  This is nonsense..He did not rape anyone

Alex:  Don't touch me..You hear me..Don't touch me

Frantz:  This is nonsense..He is not going anywhere

Detective Edwards:  Sir..You will be charged for interfering with police activities

Detective Guzman:  We need backup please..We have resistance here


_A few minutes later five squad cars arrived at Frantz's apartment and took all the guys downtown..Alex's friends were fined and released..Alex is now in jail charged with first degree rape..Frantz called Alex's mom on the phone..Let's listen:


Frantz:  Hello Mrs. Smith

Alex's Mom: Son..How are you?..Where have you been..It's been such a long time..Don't be like Alex..You have to call me sometimes..Have you seen Alex at all..I haven't heard from him in days

Frantz: I saw him this morning..In fact..The reason why I am calling is to tell you that he got arrested

Alex's Mom: He got arrested?..My son Alex?..For what?

Frantz: For rape

Alex's Mom: Rape..Never..Not my son..That's a pure lie..My son never had to force a woman for sex..Ladies love him..Where is he?

Frantz: He is downtown

Mom: I need to find him a lawyer

Frantz: I heard those guys at M,M&C are really good..I will call them when I get off the phone

Mom: How can we get him out?..I could go there and pay his bail

Frantz: He would have to see a judge first..I am going to see the guys at M,M&C to see what we can do about it

Mom: Go..Call them..Oh my god..Not my son..Let me know..Ok?

Frantz: I will

Nancy: Hello

Frantz: Hello

Nancy: What is going on babe?

Frantz: Alex got arrested

Nancy: Arrested?

Frantz: Yes

Nancy: For what?

Frantz: Rape

Nancy: Who did he rape?

Frantz: C'mon Nancy..Are you serious?..No one..It's just nonsense

Nancy: Oh my god..He needs a lawyer

Frantz: I have to go..I am going to call the guys at M,M&C

Nancy: You know my friend Beatrice knows them really well..She is friend with Marlon..Marvin and Chris

Frantz: I met them once..They are really cool guys..They have two more guys who just joined the firm recently

Nancy: You are talking about Ron and Vic..Right?

Frantz: Exactly..I am going to call them to see what they can do about Alex's situation

Nancy: Who is the victim?

Frantz: Victim?

Nancy: The alleged victim

Frantz: They did not say..They just came to my apartment and took him downtown..I will call you later..I have to call the guys now

Nancy: Ok

Receptionist:  M,M& C law firm..How can I help you?

Frantz: May I speak to a lawyer please

Receptionist: Marlon and Chris are in court..Marvin is here..You want to speak with him

Frantz: Yes please

Receptionist: Hold on please..Marvin..You have someone on line one

Marvin: What is it about?

Receptionist: I don't know

Marvin: What do you mean you don't know Linda..It could be somebody ordering pizza

Receptionist: Very funny..Here he is

Marvin: Hello..This is Marvin..How can I help you?

Frantz: Hello Marvin..How are you?..This is Frantz..You might not remember me..I met you at Sandra's birthday party

Marvin: Of course I remember you..How are you?..How is Nancy?

Frantz: You do remember

Marvin: Of course..I do have a sharp memory..How can I help you?

Frantz: My good friend Alex is in trouble..He got arrested

Marvin: For what?

Frantz: For rape

Marvin: Alex the ladies' man?..I doubt it..The ladies love him..That's bogus..Who accused him?

Frantz: I don't know yet

Marvin: Where is he?

Frantz: He is at the jail downtown

Marvin: We need to move fast..That kind of charge can really put him in danger at the jail

Frantz: How so?

Marvin: With the other inmates..He might get jumped..They don't like rapists in jail..Whether you are wrongly accused or not you could be in danger

Frantz: I see

Marvin: When the guys get back..I will talk to them about it..And early tomorrow morning..We will go downtown to see a judge and bail him out


_Later that day


Marlon: Hello

Marvin: Hey big guy..Where are you?

Marlon: We just left the court..I am so glad this case is over

Marvin: What happened?

Marlon: Mistrial

Marvin: Beautiful..Where is the player?

Marlon: Chris is right here

Chris: What do you want playboy? I am glad that case is over..Time for a vacation

Marvin: Not so fast

Chris:  What do you mean?..I did not take a break after The "I Am with You" case

Marvin:  Too bad..We have more work ahead of us

Chris:  What is it?

Marvin:  A rape case

Chris:  Rape case?

Marlon:  What did he say?..Rape case?

Chris:  Yep..Who is it?

Marlon:  The client's name is Alex

Chris:  Alex..Alex..The name sounds familiar

Marlon:  Of course you know Alex..He is friend with Nancy..He and Nancy's boyfriend are best buddies

Chris:  I think I know him..He seems to be a pretty cool guy..Rape?..I don't believe so

Marvin:  We need to go see him tomorrow and try to bail him out

Chris:  Why don't we go somewhere and talk about it..What do you think Mo?

Marlon:  Let's do that..I am starving..Tell Marvin to meet us at the Cranbury Restaurant

Chris:  No..I don't go to Cranbury..What do you know about restaurants Mo..Leave that to me..Ok

Marlon:  Whatever..He is the best tour guide in town

Marvin:  That's funny

Chris:  You heard him..Right?

Marvin:  I did..That was a good one

Chris:  Forget about Marlon's idea..Meet us at the Boucan Bleu

Marlon:  This guy is always fancy

Chris:  I am sorry..I only eat at the best places..Meet you there Marvin

Marvin:  No problem..See you guys there in a few


_At the restaurant

Marlon: Guys..Do you think we should contact Bryant..Since our client is accused of raping Jim Castillo's wife

Chris: Who is Bryant?

Marlon: C'mon man..Bryant from the "Surgeon" case..The music producer

Chris: Ok..I know Bryant very well.. For what?

Marvin: Well..Bryant is well respected in the streets..Since we are dealing with Jim Castillo..I think it's not a bad idea to have Bryant on our side

Chris: True..It makes a lot of sense..I have his number..Let me call him

Marlon: Go ahead

Chris: B..It's me..Chris

Bryant: Chris..Where have you been brother..The other day I was asking Nicole for you

Chris: Nicole?..I don't remember her..I know so many Nicole..I don't know which one you are talking about

Bryant: Nicole..She is petite..Brown eyes..Short hair style

Chris: Nicole..Now I see who you are talking about..I haven't seen her in a while my brother

Bryant: Really?..I thought you guys had a serious relationship

Chris: C'mon B..You know me better..B..We need your help

Bryant: What is going on?..Where are the guys..Where are Marlon and Marvin?

Chris: They are right here with me

Bryant: I know whenever you guys are together in a meeting..You guys must be cooking something

Chris: We are certainly cooking something

Bryant: I know..I saw you guys since "The Surgeon" case

Chris: By the way how is the doctor doing?

Bryant: He is doing fine..I got the don Bobby off his back..His business picked up..Little brother is ok

Chris: It's so good to have a big brother sometimes

Bryant: I am not a big brother to that guy..I am literally his dad..You know I paid for his medical studies..Right?

Chris: I know..I heard about it

Bryant: So..What is cooking?

Chris: What is cooking is so hot..We need your muscles

Bryant: Marvin is the muscles guys..Marvin is much bigger than I am

Chris: I know..We need your streets muscles

Bryant: Since "The Surgeon" situation with Bobby..I tried to stay as low key as possible..What is going on?

Chris: Why don't you get here B?..I don't feel comfortable talking about bit on the phone

Bryant: Really?..What could be so hot?..Where are you guys?

Chris: We are at the Boucan Bleu

Bryant: I know where that is

Chris: I know you know..Rich man

Bryant: Don't talk too loud..I don't want Uncle Sam to hear that

Chris: I know right..See you soon brother

Bryant: No problem

Marlon: What did he say?..He is coming?

Chris: Of course..He is coming

Marvin: You know Bryant is not afraid of anything

Chris: You remember Bobby was messing with his brother..The doctor..He jumped in and stopped it quick

Marvin: I know..Bryant is no joke

Marlon: Check this out..He is here already

Chris: Yep..I saw his Bentley

Marvin: Hey big guy..You got here already?..I did not recognize you..To me your Bentley was bleu

Bryant: I still have the bleu one

Chris: Excuse me..You have more than one Bentley brother

Bryant: Just four

Chris: You heard him..Just four

Marlon: Ok..Bryant..We need you..We have a case that is pretty hot..It involves Jim Castillo

Bryant: Jim Castillo..The real Jim Castillo..The Don?

Marvin: Yep

Bryant: What is it about?

Marlon: Our client is accused of raping Jim Castillo's wife

Bryant: Your client is still alive?

Marlon: Yes he is

Bryant: When last time you talk to him?

Marvin: Very funny B..The guy is fine..He is in jail

Chris: Jim would not kill him..He did not rape Jim's wife..It's just false accusation

Bryant: Where that accusation comes from?

Marlon: Well..Our client had a sexual relation with Jim Castillo's wife

Bryant: Well..That is enough reason for them to come after him

Chris: I think Jim Castillo knows that his wife is a free spirited person..This is why is not too angry about our client

Marvin: C'mon Chris..What are you saying..He is angry enough..Our guy is in prison

Marlon: So..We want to keep everything as peaceful as possible..So we call you

Bryant: In other words..You guys want me to balance the streets equation..Right?

Marlon: Exactly

Bryant: I can do that..I know a few guys in Jim Castillo's Camp

Marlon: Really?

Chris: C'mon Mo..You are talking to Bryant..Bryant is the mayor of this town

Marvin: For a minute I thought you were Chris

Chris: For a minute..The minute has expired

Bryant: Very funny guys..One of Castillo's guys..His name is Jesse..His son is an artist..We are working with him..I am in the process of signing him to my label..If something is happening..Jesse will let me know..Ok guys..I have to go..I have someone waiting for me at the office..See you guys later


_Meanwhile


Jim: Tony..How are we going to prevent Katy from being available to testify..You think it is possible to keep her drugged up all during the trial?

Tony: Well..That's pretty challenging..But..She is your wife Jim..Do you think she will go against the rape idea if she wakes up?

Jim: Definitely..She is a good person..She has a compassionate heart..There is no way she will send someone in prison on a false rape accusation..She would not do that to her worse enemy..Let alone she has feeling for that guy..She will never falsely accuse someone of rape

Tony: Women who do that are the worst of the worst..Think about it..Guys get killed in prison every day when your charge is rape..So..You are going to keep her drugged up until the trial is over

Jim: That's the plan..Will the doctor be willing to work with us?

Tony: Definitely..He is my cousin..Jim..This is pretty risky for the guy..You have to take good care of him..He might lose his license over this..And even go to prison as well

Jim: I know..Tell him that I will give him twenty stocks

Tony: Make it thirty

Jim: No problem..Thirty it is..What's a matter with you Tony?..Are you that guy agent?..You sure he is a doctor?..The way you are negotiating..It sounds like drugging people is what he does for living

Tony: One thing we must consider though

Jim: What is it?

Tony: The defense might subpoena her to testify

Jim: The doctor will just have to let them know that she is in no shape to testify

Tony: Let's hope that works

Jim: Of course..You know in court..Whatever the doctor says goes

Tony: I know


_Meanwhile at the restaurant


Marvin: I was hungry

Marlon: You had news that Whatever Bleu might run out of food or something

Chris: That's cold

Marvin: Colder than your beer..Uh

Chris: Much colder..I wish my beer was that good

Marlon: Chris..Don't make fun of him..He is your partner in food..I should send you guys to Ethiopia for a year..Where there is the famine..I think you guys would eat people

Marvin: Why not..It's survival

Chris: I know right..I would wait for them to die first

Marlon: You guys are sick

Marvin: C'mon Mo..Give the man a break..At least he would wait for them to die first

Chris: Right after the last breath though..I would get busy

Marlon: This is insane

Chris: You don't want the meat to get hard..The meat is tender when it's fresh

Marlon: How many people you have eaten already Chris?

Chris: Quite a few

Marvin: And most of them ladies..Right?

Chris: Very funny..In fact..Not most of them..All of them are beautiful ladies..Smelling good

Marlon: Guys..Let's get to talking business

Waitress: Are you ready to order?

Chris: You already know..For me it's the usual

Marlon: I will take a steak medium rare please

Marvin: I will take mine well done

Waitress: You want a steak as well..Right?

Marvin: Yes..I am not like Chris..I am not too good at cannibalism

Waitress: What do you want to drink?

Marlon: Bring me a beer as well..A very cold one

Marlon: What do you guys think of that upcoming trial?

Chris: We must win

Marvin: Without a doubt

Marlon: I hope there is evidence..Such as body fluid..So we could clear cur client from the charges

Chris: You know how it is guys..If it is a set up there will be no evidence

Marlon: Our only hope..It's to have the accuser testified in court

Marvin: There is big risk in that as well

Marlon: Credibility?

Marvin: Of course..If the client is credible that could be a problem

Chris: But..Another thing though..If she is lying..We can break her on the stand

Marvin: From what Frantz..Our client's friend told me..It's a set up..He was messing around with the guy's wife and he is accused of rape

Chris: That happened quite often..The women often out of fear would do everything the husband asked them to do

Marvin: Not only that..He was messing around with Jim Castillo's wife

Chris: What Jim Castillo?..The boss?

Marvin: Yes..That's what he said

Marlon: Ti is a very serious case

Marvin: I told you guys..But..You guys don't listen

Chris: This is serious..You think we will need security..We can bring Bryant

Marvin: Everything will be fine

_The next day at the courthouse

Marvin: Your honor..We really believe that our client deserves to be released on bail..He has no prior brushes with the law your honor..It is just a false accusation..Those are everyday occurrences your honor..Our client is a well raised individual..He is a respected member of our society..There is no way he had committed such crime your honor..Our client was not under the influence of drugs or alcohol your honor..So far your honor there is no deposition of evidences made by the prosecution..It is most likely going to be a hear say case your honor..The defense intends to bring the accuser on the stand and dig holes into the accuser's sheet of lies and prove the innocence of our client..Therefore your honor..Because of the gigantic cloud of doubt that is floating over this case..Our client should be granted bail..It is simply a case of a scorn husband..Who wants revenge and convinces or forces his wife to accuse our client of rape..We are confident that our client will be granted bail..Thank you your honor

Judge: Thank you counselor..I heard your speech in defense of your client..I must tell you upfront that I am not a fan of giving bail to rape defendants..But..In this case this is not the reason why I am not going to grant bail to your client..I was informed that the accuser is the wife of a very notorious man in town..He is not notorious for his kindness..He is notorious for his ability to manipulate the streets..Therefore..I chose to not grant bail to your client for his own safety

Marvin: With all due respect your honor..I must inform you that jail is not a safe place either when you are accused of rape

Judge: I understand that..But I can arrange for him to be safe while in custody here..But we cannot guarantee his safety while on the streets

Marlon: Your honor..We appreciate your concern and the effort and actions you would take to assure his safety..But..Our client will be better being with his family during this difficult time your honor..Also ..It will be better..A more adequate situation to prepare for the upcoming trial

Judge: I hear you counselor..But you have not mentioned anything regarding the safety of Mr. Smith..This is my concern..This is the reason why I am denying bail to your client..This is not because I want to keep him in jail..It is a safety issue

Chris: We understand that and we once again appreciate your concern your honor..But..The defense is willing and prepared to take the proper measures to protect Mr. Smith

Judge: This is not a guarantee..People have been attacked in the past..And even lawyers..Therefore..Your client being under the protection of the sheriff department will be better..This is what I think..At least for the duration of the trial

Marvin: Your honor..This is the point I was about to make..After the trial..Our client will not hide in a hole..I don't see why not being in the streets now

Judge: I hear you counselor ..My decision is final..No bail

Marvin: Thank you your honor

Judge: Just work fast to bring the case to trial as soon as you can..That would reduce the time that your client has to spend in jail

Marlon: This is what we intend to do your honor


_The next day..The guys visit Alex in jail to prepare for the upcoming trial


C.O.: Please sit at table fifteen..It's a much larger table

Marvin: You are getting tired of seeing us here..Aren't you?

C.O.: Not really..In fact I am still looking forward to find you guys a room here

Marlon: You are going to wait for a long time officer Neil

Chris: An eternity I should say

C.O.: Where is the love?..I have a feeling no one wants to be here with me?

Chris: We will visit you often..How about that?

C.O.: Fair enough..Your client will be brought down soon

Marlon: Thank you

Chris: Good morning

Alex: Good morning

Marlon: How are you Alex?

Alex: I feel much better that I see you guys here

Marvin: It's a very scary place..Isn't it?

Chris: Trust me..This guy knows this place too well

Alex: Really?..You have been locked up before?

Marvin: Yes sir..I served nine long years

Alex: For what?

Chris: For murder..He is a better criminal than you

Marvin: Yep..I guess so..If it was not for this guy..My brother Marlon..I would still be in there

Marlon: Me..Yet..He does not appreciate it

Alex: You were innocent..Right?

Chris: No..He killed someone

Marvin: So..I know too well that you don't have to be guilty to be behind bars..That was my motivation to become a lawyer when I got out

Marlon: Why do you think you are accused of rape Alex?..You should know

Alex: I do know..I was messing around with Jim Castillo's wife..We got caught doing so and he forced her to accuse me of rape

Marvin: Do you think she is the type of person that would willingly go along with such thing?

Alex: Not at all..She is a great person..She was bored and she wanted some adventure..She really likes me..I was with her the day before I was arrested

Chris: So..You don't think she would testify for the prosecution..Is that what I am hearing?

Alex: Definitely not..She would never falsely accuse someone of rape..She is just not that type of person

Marlon: You think it would be safe to have her on the stand?

Alex: Totally

Chris: If she is willing to testify on your behalf..You will be fine

Marvin: That's what we are hoping

Marlon: We want to let you know that we intend to go to court next week..The sooner the better

Alex: Fine with me..You guys talked to my parents

Marvin: They called the office..The office is in constant communication with them..Next week..We will start the fight..And you will get your freedom back

Marlon: We are sorry..That we could not get you bail..The judge indicated that he prefers you being in there for safety reason

Alex:  There is no safety here

Marvin:  I know right..The judge needs to spend some times in jail

Marlon:  Anyway..I think he made sense..Outside is not always that safe in such situation

Chris:  I disagree..After the trial he has to walk the streets..Anyway..You will be out soon

Alex:  I hope so

Marlon:  We are leaving now..We will keep you posted

Alex:  Thanks guys


_A day after..Marvin called Alex's friend on the phone


Frantz:  Hello

Marvin:  Hello Frantz..How are you..This is Marvin from the law firm

Frantz:  How are you Marvin?

Marvin:  Great

Frantz:  Have you guys talked to Alex?

Marvin:  Yes..We visited him yesterday..He is in good spirit..He is ready to fight for his freedom..He is ready to prove his innocence

Frantz:  I know..What happened is..They could not muscle him in so they are trying to use another avenue..Alex did not rape anyone

Marvin:  I believe you..You are friend with the lady..Right?

Frantz:  Who are you referring to?

Marvin:  The alleged victim

Frantz:  Katy?..We are not friends..We met a couple times..She came to my place once to meet Alex

Marvin:  Do you have it on video?

Frantz:  No..She did not stay..She came to pick him up to go somewhere

Marvin:  Would you be able to talk to her and ask her to testify for the defense

Frantz: I don't think it is possible..I don't have her phone number..I don't think it would be safe for her..Even her female friends stop talking to her..They fear that the guys would retaliate against them..I am right now on Jim Castillo's black list

Marvin: How so?

Frantz: Alex and I had a little encounter with Jim's guys at the mall

Marvin: It seems she will have to be subpoenaed in order for her to come to court

Frantz: I really think so..She would not testify for the defense willingly..She would be killed

Marvin: I see..We have to subpoena her..Ok..Thanks Frantz..We will see you soon..The trial is for next week if all goes well

Frantz: I will be there..I will take time off from work to be there every day

Marvin: Later


_Meanwhile at the Castillo's home


Housekeeper: Sir..The doctor is here

Jim: Tell him to come upstairs

Dr. Angelo: Hi Jim..I thought you were sleeping

Jim: She woke up this morning..She was talking..She asked for food

Dr.: If she asked for food give her food

Jim: I did..I told one of the ladies to prepare a soup for her

Dr. Angelo: Good

Jim: Can you give her a stronger dose..So..She could sleep longer

Dr. Angelo: I can't do that..She could die..If she wakes up and being really alert..Call me and I will come and give her more..Where is she now?

Jim: She is in the room..Come with me

Katy: Leave me alone..Please..You are poisoning me

Jim: How come her voice is so low?

Dr. Angelo: It's the effect of the drugs..She does not have much energy to talk loud..She is sedated

Katy: Please..Leave me alone..I want to talk to my friends..Please leave me alone..I don't want shots

Dr. Angelo: This is good for you..It will help you relax so you can sleep

Jim: You gave it to her

Dr. Angelo: I did..She is sleeping already

Jim: Great..I want you to give it to her every day until the trial is over..I don't want her to realize that the guy Alex is in jail for rape

Dr. Angelo: You think she will oppose to that?

Jim: Definitely..I know what kind of person she is..She is against injustice

Dr. Angelo: She did you wrong

Jim: She is a free spirited person..She just wanted to have fun..She is that crazy..She does what she wants..I don't think she does not love me..But she believes one can be romantically involved with more than persons

Dr. Angelo: Ok..She is very different..Therefore..We should keep her drugged till the end of the trial

Jim: At least that is the plan


_Meanwhile..Jim's friends were still at work to prove their loyalty to their boss..Frantz phone rings..Let's listen


Frantz: Hello

Jim's guy: Hello

Frantz: Who is this?

Jim's guy: It's us..You guys violate us big time..It is time to pay

Frantz: Who are you?

Jim's guy: Listen to me..We ask the questions..See where your disrespecting friend is now..Well..We are not done

Frantz: I don't know what you are talking about..It seems that you guys did not get the message we sent you

Jim's guy: You see what happened to your friend..See where he is now?..Now it's your turn to pay

Frantz: You are wasting your time

Jim's guy: Do you know who we work for?..Do you know who Castillo is?..Have you heard of Jim Castillo?

Frantz: I heard too much about him already..This is why I want you to get off my phone

Jim's guy: You will see

Frantz: Get off my phone..Good bye


_The next day Frantz takes Nancy shopping and they are on their way back home..Let's listen:


Frantz: That car has been on my bumper since we left the mall

Nancy: Which one?

Frantz: The gray Benz..I am going to turn right onto the next street..I want to see what they do

Nancy: They turned as well

Frantz: They are following me..I will make a u-turn right here and see

Nancy: They are making a u-turn as well

Frantz: Babe..Put on your seatbelt..Brace yourself..When I reach Franklin..I will turn right

Nancy: You are doing ninety miles an hour

Frantz: Don't worry..I will downshift and do a compression..I will go from fifth to third and then second..It's coming

Nancy: Oh my god..Oh my god..Oh my god

Frantz: You are fine..You are fine..They did not make the turn..They went straight

Nancy: What are you doing?

Frantz: I am making a u-turn

Nancy: You are back toward them?

Frantz: They are going to turn on the next street..They probably think we are going straight down Franklin

Nancy: The light is red

Frantz: I have to take it..You see any sign of them?

Nancy: I think you lost them

Frantz: I going to your place..They know where I live..They could go there and wait for me

Nancy: Babe..We should call the police

Frantz: No..We are not calling the police..We are going to handle the situation

Nancy: Your phone is ringing

Frantz: Hello

Jeff: Hello..What's up big guy..I passed by your place..I did not see your car

Frantz: I did not go home..I was in a pursuit

Jeff: What do you mean?

Frantz: I was being followed by a car

Jeff: Followed by a car..You are being paranoid

Frantz: Not at all..Nancy was with me..I had to do some serious maneuvers to shake them off

Jeff: This is more serious than we think

Frantz: Jeff..Can it be more serious than that?..Alex is in Jail..Those guys confronted me more than twice

Jeff: Why would they be after you though?

Frantz: Jim Castillo has a GPS record that his wife was at my house

Jeff: Was she at your apartment?

Frantz: Yes she was

Jeff: Where was I?

Frantz: You were not there that day

Jeff: If she was at your place..You are fully involved..How is Alex doing?

Frantz: He is ok..But he is in jail for no reason at all..Today..I will drop by to see him

Jeff: Pick me up..I will go with you

Frantz: No problem


_Later that day Frantz and Jeff went to the jail to visit Alex


C.O.: Table eleven please

Frantz: Thank you

Jeff: I see him

Frantz: I did not recognize him..He let his beard grow

Alex: What's going on guys?

Frantz: How are you big guy?

Alex: I am ok..Can't wait to go home..What's up Jeff

Jeff: I am ok..Just stop by to see you

Alex: I appreciate that

Frantz: What's up with the beard?

Alex: I did not feel like shaving every morning..So I let it grow

Frantz: I thought you were hiding from Jim Castillo

Jeff: He knows where you are

Alex: You guys know me better than that..You guys need to grow a beard to hide from him

Frantz: How is the situation here for you?

Alex: I am ok..My lawyers put me in solitary to protect me..I was fine in general population

Frantz: Ok..Tough guy..Once they find out that you are here for rape..Things can change

Alex: Not really..They know I am here for rape..But they know the story as well..They saw it in the news

Jeff: So you are like a super star in there

Alex: I don't know about that..Frantz..My man I am sorry..You warned me so much about the whole thing

Frantz: Don't worry about it now..It's too late for that..When you are in the middle of a war..It is no time to question why you signed up for service

Alex: Robert told me that you were in a pursuit

Frantz: Yes..I shook them off

Alex: One thing Frantz does well it's driving..I really think he should have been a race car driver

Frantz: Thanks but no thanks..Car racing is too dangerous for me..On a more serious note..The trial starts in a couple of days..Are you ready?

Alex: Of course I am

Jeff: The man has no choice


_Finally the day of the trial has arrived..It was a cold morning..The defense lawyers met outside the courthouse fifteen minutes before the trial..Alex's family arrived there a couple minutes after..All his friends were there to support him including Frantz and his girlfriend Nancy..The prosecution team arrived two minutes before nine..At nine O'clock both parties walked into the courtroom..The gallery was crowded..The public wanted to be there..The case was about the guy who raped Jim Castillo's wife..Everybody saw him as a dead man walking..Jim Castillo soon walked into the courtroom with six guys wearing suit around him..They were all wearing dark sun glasses..Alex was there chatting with his lawyers..Did not show any sign of nervousness..All his friends and family were sitting right behind him..Fifteen minutes after the courtroom door opened..The judge walked into the courtroom..And a loud voice filled the room


Bailiff: All rise..This courtroom is now in session


-Guys..My readers..This is the time we have been waiting for..Let's go in the courtroom before they close the doors


Judge: Have a seat everyone..Today is the beginning of the trial of the state against Alex Smith..We have pretty much a crowded courtroom here..I expect everyone to be at their best behavior..I don't want any talking in my courtroom..No moving around..If you need to use the restroom..Do it now..I expect everything to go pretty smoothly through the entire trial..Having said that..Both parties are present?

Marvin: Yes your honor

Prosecutor: Yes your honor

Judge: Good..Defendant..Stand up please..How do you plead against the charges

Alex: Not guilty your honor

Judge: Counselor..Have you provided all information to your client regarding the charges?

Marlon: Yes your honor

Judge: Prosecutor..Are you ready to start your opening statement?

Prosecutor: Yes your honor..The prosecution will need a few minutes your honor

Judge: Somebody is not prepared

Prosecutor: We are ready your honor..The opening statement is in a folder and the folder is left in the car outside

Judge: You want the defense to start your opening for you

Chris: We will gladly help the prosecution your honor

Judge: You heard that prosecutor

Prosecutor: We heard that your honor..The prosecution team does not need any help from the defense your honor..Your honor the folder has arrived

Judge: Order please..You may start whenever you are ready sir

Prosecutor: Thank you your honor..Good morning ladies and gentlemen..Today we are here to bring justice to a victim..A young woman who is so affected by the crime committed against her..She cannot be in this courtroom..You the people of the jury have the duty today to be the voice for that young woman..That young wife..This case is very personal to me..I believe that the people such as the defendant Alex Smith who committed such crimes should not walk our streets..Here we have an innocent young lady..A married woman who is trying to live a peaceful life with her husband..The defendant found nothing else to do but to rape her..Those are the people that our society should really get rid of..God knows how many people he had already raped

Elise: Objection your honor

Judge: Sustained

Elise: Your honor..The defense is desperately trying to paint a portrait of my client which is far from being accurate..Our client is not a rapist your honor..He is a decent young man..Another young man being accused of a crime that he did not commit..For the defense to insinuated that our client is a serial rapist is unacceptable

Judge: I hear you counselor ..Your point is well taken..But it is only an opening statement

Marlon: Your honor..We understand that it is an opening statement..An opening statement is all the prosecution needs to poison the mind of the jury

Judge: I understand..The prosecution should refrain on the insinuation..And must remember that the defendant is innocent until proven guilty..Understood?

Prosecutor: Yes your honor

Judge: You may proceed

Prosecutor: Thank you your honor..I understand that we must respect the rights of the defendant..We must not forget that the victim human right was violated..She was forced to perform a sexual act..Maybe she was drugged..Maybe she was put to sleep..Your honor those who have committed sexual crimes are the worse human being of our society..If we stand by and watch and do nothing we are as well rapists..If we think such acts are entertainments..We are nothing but a bunch of rapists disguised as spectators..Therefore your honor..This is no time to accept sexual crimes as a form of entertainment..We must stop being hypocrites and call it what it is..Rape against anyone should be considered as a terrible violation and should be dealt with accordingly..If you stand by and watch and do nothing..You look in the mirror..You are in fact looking at a rapist..You are a rapist..Those who observed the abuse and do nothing are worse than the one perpetuating the abuse..Therefore ladies and gentlemen of the jury..You have an important duty today..That is not to be a passive rapist by finding the defendant guilty of all counts..I am not going to talk much longer..There is no need to do so..Because a rape crime against one is a crime against all..The prosecution will rest assured at the end of this trial..The defendant..That monster

Chris: Objection your honor

Judge: Sustained

Chris: Your honor..Once again the prosecutor is using his defamation brush..Our client is far for being a monster..The prosecution is in fact behaving like a monster by constantly trying to eat away our client Character

Prosecutor: I am the monster..I am not the one who forced himself inside Jim Castillo's wife..How am I the monster?

Chris: If someone forced himself inside Mr. Castillo's wife..It was not our client

Judge: Order please..No exchange among the two parties on my floor..You are not here to address each other..You are here to address the court..Prosecutor..Proceed please..Last warning prosecutor..Do not use defamatory adjectives when you are referring to the defendant

Prosecutor: Understood your honor

Judge: Proceed

Prosecutor: Thank you your honor..I simple intend to say to the good people of the jury..To make sure justice is rendered to the Castillo family..To make sure justice is rendered to that young wife..Who is so badly shaken and embarrassed..Could not make it to court today..Be a voice for her..Send a clear message to the defendant by finding him guilty on all counts..Thank you your honor

Judge: Thank you..The defense has the floor

Marvin: Thank you your honor..Good morning Ladies and gentlemen for the jury..Today is a very sad day..Today is a sad day simply because..This is two thousand sixteen..There should not have been room for such injustice in our lives..Too many times we witness our young men go to prison for very long period of time for rape..Rape they did not commit..To find later..After serving twenty five years behind bars that they were innocent..This is something..This is a mindset..This is a practice..This is an injustice that must be stopped..I am standing before you today with a heart full of sadness..Simply because I know for fact that our client is innocent..He did not rape Mrs. Castillo..Yet..The claws of injustice are tightening around him and getting ready to drag him into the world of men falsely accused of rape..It is with a heart filled of chagrin that I must stand before you and deliver this speech..A speech that is much too late to save the lives of so many young men..Young men who were full of great expectation just like our clients..I also feel a great sense of shame and guilt for being a member of our society and to not have done something sooner to change the situation..Today we all here have a chance to redeem ourselves..Today..We are all presented with an opportunity to do better..We are presented with the opportunity to say no to that usual occurrence that has devastated the lives of many..Now is the time where we must stand together to say no as one voice against that injustice..Now is the time to stand and say never again..Our sons ..Grandsons..Brothers..Cousins..Uncles..Fathers should go to prison for crimes they did not commit..Today..Ladies and gentlemen..Technology brought great relief and clarity into that matter with the help of DNA..Before the DNA era..It was regular practice to send a young man to jail just because someone accused him of rape..Today..In this case..We seemed to have travelled in the past..Because..Ladies d and gentlemen there is no DNA involved in the case..Somehow no DNA evidence was collected..Therefore it is back to the usual practice of she said..Nevertheless..We the defense..We are confident that at the end of this trial..We will make it clear enough that our client did not rape Mrs. Castillo..We will prove to you that this is another attempt to destroy another young man's life..We are confident that you the good people of this jury will see through the cloud of injustice and find our client not guilty on all counts..We are looking forward to that day..We are looking forward to that day because we are tired of the triumph of injustice..We are looking forward to that day because we are tired of mothers lamenting due to the lost of their sons..We are looking forward to that day where justice will triumph..We care looking forward to that day where this jury will find our client not guilty..That day where he will be released to his family and get back to his duty of being a great contributor to our society..We are looking forward to that day where Mr. Alex Smith will be found not guilty on all counts..Thank you your honor

Judge: Thank you sir..It is always a pleasure to hear the guys from M,M&C deliver a statement

Marvin: Thank you your honor

Judge: Why you guys never used written statement?

Marvin: Your honor..We all feel it's always better to talk from the heart

Judge: You guys are extremely gifted

Marvin: Thank you your honor

Judge: You are welcome..At this time the court will adjourn for lunch..Please remain seated until the jury leaves the room


_During lunch time the guys are talking


Marlon: Great job Marvin

Marvin: Thank you brother

Chris: I did not know Marvin could do such a great job

Marlon: Chris is joking Marv..He knows better

Marvin: I was about to ask him..Where have you been during "The Family" case

Chris: I know..I know..I know what you are capable of..I have seen you preaching to the ladies

Marvin: Very funny

Marlon: That's where you guys do your practice by preaching to the ladies

Marvin: You should know brother

Marlon: Me?..I am a married man

Chris: Marlon always hide behind his marriage

Marvin: Right..Right..As if he was born married

Marvin: He was such a player..I went to prison because of one of his girls..I walked her home after a party we had at our house..The police arrested me..They were looking for some dude

Marlon: Well..Tell the whole story..You had sex with my girlfriend that night too

Marvin: I don't know what you are talking about

Marlon: You should know..All of the sudden you lost memory

Marvin: You are not over that yet brother

Waitress: Are you guys ready to order?

Marvin: Yes..Please..Bring some food here..That man is about to kill me

Marlon: How do you guys see the prosecution this afternoon

Chris: They will introduce a witness..I don't think they will find more than two witnesses

Marvin: We have to get ready..They might bring someone coached to lie on the stand

Marlon: We definitely have to be vigilant

Chris: We must not forget this whole case is based on lie..Our client did not rape anybody

Marvin: This is one of the best steaks I had eaten

Chris: Really?..You need to go out with me more often Marv

Marvin: C'mon Chris..That was pretty good

Marlon: I got you guys..I will pay

Chris: No problem..Thanks..Dinner is on me

Marvin: I will leave the tip for her

Waitress: You guys enjoyed the food

Marvin: It was fantastic

Waitress: I am happy that you love it

Marvin: It was well done..Juicy..The best I had..What is your name?

Waitress: Irene

Marvin: You are new here?

Waitress: Yes..I am a student..I work here part time

Marvin: What is your major?

Waitress: Criminal justice..I intend to become a lawyer as well

Marvin: Great..This is for you

Waitress: For me..You want change?

Marvin: No..Keep it..It's yours

Waitress: Thanks..See you guys later

Marlon: Guys..Let's go..It's almost that time

Chris: Marlon..Did you see that?

Marlon: What?

Chris: Marvin gave the waitress a Benjamin for tip

Marlon: What's a Benjamin?

Chris: A hundred dollar bill..You know he is looking for something else

Marvin: C'mon Chris..She is a student..She might need it

Chris: She is a student..She is fine too

Marvin: I am not going to deny that..Yes..She is

Marlon: You guys are so crazy..It's all about the ladies..Guys we are here..Get ready

Chris: What are you saying Mo..We are ready


Bailiff: All rise..This court is now in session

Judge: Thank you..Have a seat everyone..I hope everybody had a good lunch

Marvin: I had the best steak you honor

Judge: You had what?

Marvin: The best steak

Judge: Really?..At the Mirage restaurant

Marvin: Yes

Judge: They are pretty good there..I tried it before..So..You are ready?

Marvin: Yes we are your honor

Judge: We are done with opening statements.. At this time..The prosecution may introduce its first witness..Prosecution..Are you ready?

Prosecutor: Yes we are your honor

Judge: Yes your honor..At this time the prosecution would like to call Miss Claudette Palmer

Bailiff: State your name for the court please

Witness: Claudette..Claudette palmer

Bailiff: Raise your right hand and repeat after me..I swear to tell the truth..Nothing but the truth

Witness: I swear to tell the truth..Nothing but the truth

Judge: Have a seat lease Miss Palmer

Prosecutor: Good afternoon Miss Palmer

Witness: Good afternoon sir

Prosecutor: Miss Palmer..We really appreciate it that you take the time off your schedule to be here

Witness: No problem..I was off today anyway

Prosecutor: Miss Palmer..What do you do?

Witness: I am a chef

Prosecutor: How long you've been a chef Miss Palmer?

Witness: For fifteen years sir

Prosecutor: Miss. Palmer..You work for the Castillo family..Do you not?

Witness: Yes I do

Prosecutor: Miss Palmer..Have you seen the defendant before?

Witness: I think so

Marlon: Objection your honor

Judge: Sustained

Marlon: Your honor..The witness is not sure whether she sees our client before..It should be a yes or a no..I think I see her before as well

Judge: Yes or no ma'am..Have you seen the defendant before?

Witness: Yes I have

Prosecutor: Thank you your honor..Where have you seen the defendant?

Witness: At the Castillo's residence

Prosecutor: When and in what circumstance you have seen the defendant?

Witness: The defendant walked into the kitchen and opened the fridge door and took two drinks out of the fridge

Prosecutor: Did you talk to the defendant at that time?

Witness: No I did not

Prosecutor: You thought the defendant was a guess..Did you not?

Witness: Yes

Prosecutor: The defendant could have been an intruder..Could he be not?

Marvin: Objection your honor

Judge: Sustained

Marvin: Your honor..Once again the prosecutor is asking the witness to guess

Judge: Prosecutor..You said could have been..Rephrase your question please

Prosecutor: Miss Palmer You did not know whether the defendant was a guess or not..Did you Miss Palmer?

Witness: No I did not

Prosecutor: You would not know the defendant had just raped Mrs. Castillo..Would you?

Chris: Objection

Judge: The witness may answer the question..The defense can challenge those questions during cross examination..The prosecution may proceed

Prosecutor: Thank you your honor..The defendant is and could in fact be the one who raped Mrs. Castillo..Could he be not

Witness: Yes

Prosecutor: No further questions your honor

Judge: The defense may now cross examine the witness

Marvin: Thank you your honor..Miss. Palmer..You indicated that you saw the defendant at the Castillo's residence..Did you not?

Witness: Yes sir

Marvin: You also stated that the defendant came downstairs and grabbed drinks from the fridge?..Did you not ma'am?

Witness: Yes

Marvin: How many drinks did he take from the fridge that one time ma'am?

Witness: He took two drinks

Marvin: Two drinks..That would indicate that the defendant was taking a drink for someone else..Would it not?

Prosecutor: Objection

Judge: The witness may answer the question

Marvin: Would it not?

Witness: There could be..Or..He might have been very thirsty

Marvin: Great point Miss Palmer..The defendant to take two drinks from the fridge for himself..He might have been very thirsty..Therefore..My next question is..Was the defendant agitated..Was he sweating..Or..Breathing hard?

Witness: No sir

Marvin: None of the above..So..He had a very calm demeanor when he came downstairs..Did he not Miss Palmer?

Witness: You can say that

Marvin: Yes or no please..He had a calm demeanor?

Witness: Yes

Marvin: No further questions your honor

Marlon: Go ahead Chris

Marvin: I want to yield the floor to my colleague

Judge: Proceed please

Chris: Miss. Palmer..Right?..Did I pronounce your name right?

Witness: Yes you did sir

Chris: Thank you..Miss Palmer..During that time you were cooking in the kitchen..Did you hear any noise of two people fighting upstairs?

Witness: No sir

Chris: Did you hear any noise of struggle..Stumping..What have you..During that time ma'am?

Witness: No sir

Chris: Did you hear any noise that would suggest someone was laughing upstairs?

Witness: I might have heard laughing upstairs

Prosecutor: Objection your honor

Judge: Sustained

Prosecutor: Your honor..The witness does not remember..Has no clear memory of hearing laughter

Judge: Ma'am..Did you hear laughter or not?

Witness: I am not sure your honor

Judge: The defense may proceed

Chris: Miss Palmer..Did the menu vary on the day that you saw the defendant at the Castillo's home?

Witness: Yes sir

Chris: Miss. Palmer..Can you elaborate for the court in what way the menu had changed that day?

Witness: Mrs. Castillo usually eats chicken salad for lunch..That day I saw the defendant in the house..She had ordered me to make three different dishes

Chris: Do you recall what those dishes were Miss Palmer?

Prosecutor: Objection

Judge: Sustained

Prosecutor: Your honor..The defense is asking questions that have nothing to do to the facts regarding this case..Whether Miss Castillo wanted to eat more food that day is far from being a reason to get raped

Chris: Your honor..The prosecutor is playing the dumb card here..Thinking he is slick enough to fool the court

Judge: Defense..Do you have valuable reason for going that route?..Are you trying to prove a point?

Chris: Yes your honor..I am trying to prove a point..I want the court to understand that Miss Castillo ordered and added the new dishes to the menu because our client was her guest on that day

Prosecution: Objection

Judge: Overruled..The defense may proceed

Chris: Thank you your honor..Miss Palmer..You've been cooking for Mrs. Castillo for quite sometimes..Have you not?

Witness: Yes sir

Chris: During that long period of time..Have Mrs. Castillo ever asked you to prepare dishes other than her chicken salad for lunch?

Witness: No sir..Not for herself..Only when she has guests

Chris: Therefore ma'am..Miss Castillo asked you for more food..Simply suggested that she had a guest with her that day..Did it not?

Prosecutor: Objection

Judge: Overruled

Chris: That suggested that Mrs. Castillo had a guest with her..Did it not ma'am?

Witness: I would say so

Chris: Yes or no ma'am..That suggested that Miss Castillo had a guest with her that day..Did it not?

Witness: Yes sir

Chris: No further questions your honor

Judge: The prosecution can now do a redirect if it chooses to

Prosecutor: Thank you your honor..Miss Palmer..You are not sure that Mrs. Castillo had a guest with her that day..Are you Miss Palmer?

Witness: No sir

Prosecutor: The defendant could have been an intruder..Could he not

Marlon: Objection

Judge: Sustained

Marlon: Your honor..Here we go again..The prosecutor with the "could" questions..We already prove that our client was not an intruder..He was simply a guest at the Castillo's home

Judge: You may proceed with the redirect prosecutor

Prosecutor: No further questions your honor

Judge: Thank you..The prosecution may now call its second witness


_Meanwhile


Giselle: Hello

Martine: How are you Giselle?

Giselle: I am fine..Have you heard from Katy at all?

Martine: No..It's been almost a week since I spoke with her

Giselle: I know the guys don't want us to speak much to her..But..She is our friend..We can't abandon her completely

Martine: You are so right..I understand she made a terrible mistake for cheating on Jim..But..This is not a reason to isolate her

Giselle: I know..I don't care what the guys say..I am going to go over there and see how she is doing

Martine: I called her yesterday..She did not answer the phone..It did not ring at all..It seemed that her phone is off

Giselle: Something is happening..I am on my way there..You want to come along

Martine: Sure..Pick me up..My husband will kill me if he finds out that I was at Katy's house

Giselle: We cannot be like cowards and let those guys do whatever they want to her..She is our friend

Martine: Let me get dressed

Giselle: You are always naked

Martine: No..I was not..I had shorts on

Giselle: I will be there in ten minutes

Martine: No problem


_Twenty five minutes later..Giselle and Martine were at the Castillo's residence to visit their friend Katy

Giselle: Hello..How are you?

Housekeeper: Good morning ma'am

Giselle: Where is Katy?

Housekeeper: Mrs. Castillo is in her room..She has not been too well the past few days..She does not come down at all

Giselle: What do you mean?

Housekeeper: It is almost a week she has not been downstairs

Martine: Really?..What's wrong with her?

Housekeeper: I don't know ma'am

Giselle: KATY..KATY..KATY..Where are you?..KATY..KATY..Don't play with me..Answer me..It's me Giselle..Martine is with me as well..Where are you Katy

Martine: Open the door

Giselle: Katy..Katy..You are sleeping at this time..It's twelve o'clock..Wake up Katy..Oh my god..You are a mess..Look at your hair

Martine: Katy..What's wrong baby?..Talk to me..Talk to me baby..What happened to you?

Giselle: Martine..Go to the bathroom get some water for me..Let's wash her face..Wake up girl..Look at you?..Wash her face Martine

Martine: Wake up baby..It's me Martine..What happened to you?

Katy: I don't know..I am tired..I need to sleep

Giselle: Did you take any pills Katy?..Tell me..Tell your sister..What kind of drugs you took baby?

Katy: The d..Doc..Doctor

Martine: What doctor baby?..Talk to me

Giselle: Something is fishy here..Martine..Go and call the housekeeper for me

Martine: Come with me

Housekeeper: I am not allowed to go inside the bedroom

Giselle: Come here..Listen to me..Have you seen a doctor coming here?

Housekeeper:  Yes..The doctor comes here every day to check on Mrs. Castillo

Martine:  Really?

Housekeeper:  Short visits..He usually leaves in fifteen minutes

Giselle:  I see..Thank you..Martine..Katy is being drugged

Martine:  Why would they do that though?

Giselle:  I don't know..That's not right..But..Remember..What she did could have gotten her killed

Martine:  Why drugging her?

Giselle:  I got it..They probably don't want her to get involved in the trial

Martine:  You are so right..But..She did not have to get involved

Giselle:  If the court had subpoenaed her..She would have no choice or be held in contempt

Martine:  Wow..We have to do something Giselle

Giselle:  Look at her skin..Her hair..She has not taken a bath for days

Martine:  She lost so much weight..Is she eating at all?

Giselle:  I don't know..My friend is such an elegant woman..Look at her

Martine:  What are we going to do?

Giselle:  Let's look around..Maybe the drug the doctor is using is here..Somewhere in the house

Martine:  Look..You are right Giselle..It's in this closet

Giselle:  Oh my god..It's a whole pharmacy in here..Look..There are some vitamins there as well

Martine:  Let's switch the tags..The doctor with give vitamins instead of the drugs

Giselle:  You are right..The bottles look exactly the same

Martine:  Hurry up..The doctor's name is here as well

Giselle:  I know that guy..He is friend with my husband

Martine:  Really?

Giselle:  He is not going to come here for long

Martine:  What do you plan on doing?

Giselle: I am going to tell my brother to get him

Martine: You think he would do it?

Giselle: Of course..He is totally against injustice..Let wash her up a bit before we go..And give her some food

Martine: No problem..She is up..Not up..Her eyes are open

Giselle: We have to coach her..She has to behave as if she is drugged when the doctor give her the vitamin tomorrow

Martine: Katy..Can you see me?

Katy: Yes

Martine: What is my name?

Katy: I don't know..I don't remember

Giselle: Listen to me Kat..We switched the drug bottles' labels with the vitamins..Tomorrow you will not be drugged..But you have to act like it

Katy: Act like what?

Giselle: Good..You are here with me..Act as if you are drugged..I will take care of the evil doctor soon


_Meanwhile in the courtroom


Judge: The prosecution may call its second witness

Prosecutor: Your honor..The prosecution wants to introduce a video for the record

Marlon: Your honor..The defense was not informed about the video

Prosecutor: Your honor..We did sent a copy to the defense

Marlon: Your honor..We received the copy of the video late last night..Our expert did not have time to properly analyze the video

Judge: Around what time did the defense receive the video?

Marvin: It was around eight in the evening your honor

Judge: It did not arrive early..But I don't think it was late..I think form eight o'clock till court time is enough time to analyze a video..How long is the video?

Prosecutor: It is only seven minutes long your honor

Judge: You had time to analyze fifteen seven minutes videos..Therefore..I think the video should be introduced as evidence

Prosecutor: Thank you your honor..In this frame..You can clearly see the defendant walking around the Castillo's home..Looking agitated and seemed to be searching for something

Chris: Objection

Judge: Sustained

Chris: Your honor..The prosecutor is assuming..He said that our client seemed to be looking for something..He does not know at all about what our client is doing

Judge: Prosecutor may proceed

Prosecutor: Your honor..You can see him in this frame right here with no shirt on..Clearly a bit sweaty..As if he has been in some type of struggle

Marvin: Objection your honor

Judge: Counselor..You will have a chance to do a cross examination..Prosecution may proceed

Prosecutor: Finally your honor..Here's the defendant lying next to Mrs. Castillo..She seems to be unconscious in that frame..I would like this video to be introduced as evidence for the record..Thank you your honor

Judge: This exhibit will be introduced as evidence for the record..The defense may now do a cross examination

Marvin: Thank you your honor..I want the jury to understand..Those are clips taken from a very long video..The prosecution edited the video to fit their needs..They edit the video in a way to incriminate our client..For instance..They show sweat on our client body..But did not show how he got sweaty..They show Mrs. Castillo Taking a nap but did not show why she got tired and was taking a nap..This is designed purposely to create insinuation in the mind of the jury..But..The defense is confident that the jury members are more clever than the prosecutor thinks..Thank you honor

Judge: Thank you..We are moving right along..The prosecution may now introduce its next witness

Prosecution: Your honor..The prosecution will rest

Judge: The defense may now call its first witness

Marlon: Thank you your honor..Your honor..The court issued a subpoena for Mrs. Castillo to testify..We did not hear anything from the prosecution

Prosecutor: Your honor..The prosecution is aware of the subpoena...But Mrs. Castillo cannot take the stand due to her health condition..She is heavily sedated due..She is still shaking up due to the attack

Marlon: Your honor..The defense will therefore call the doctor who is taking care of Mrs. Castillo

Judge: Is the doctor present?

Marlon: No..Your honor..We would like the court to issue an urgent subpoena in order to have the doctor here this afternoon

Judge: I made note of it counselor

Marlon: Thank you your honor


_Later that afternoon


Marvin: Your honor..The defense would like to call Dr. Angelo Evanoche to the Stand

Bailiff: Raise your right hand and repeat after me..I swear to tell the truth..Nothing but the truth

Witness: I swear to tell the truth..Nothing but the truth

Judge: Have a seat sir

Marvin: Doctor..How are you today?

Witness: I am fine..Thank you

Marvin: Doctor..Mrs. Castillo has been at under your care for the last two weeks..Has she not?

Witness: Yes sir

Marvin: Can Mrs. Castillo take the stand?

Doctor: No she cannot

Marvin: She is heavily sedated

Marvin: Doctor..She cannot take the stand because she sedated..Am I right?

Doctor: yes

Marvin: Besides being sedated Doctor..There is no other reason that would prevent her from taking the stand..Yes or no Doctor?

Doctor: No

Marvin: Doctor..Who is getting her sedated?

Doctor: I am

Marvin: Why you are getting her sedated Doctor?

Doctor: She needed to rest..She needed a break from all the stress from the event

Marvin: Who recommend the sedation Doctor?

Doctor: It was recommended by her husband

Marvin: No further questions your honor

Judge: The prosecution may cross examine the witness

Prosecutor: The prosecution has no questions for Doctor Evanoche

Judge: Thank you..The court will now adjourn for the day..The court will reconvene tomorrow at nine o'clock..Please remain seated until the jury leaves the room..Have a good night everyone


_The next morning


Marlon: Guys..Today is the day..We are going to call Alex on the stand..Do you think it's a good idea?

Marvin: Why not?

Chris: Not so fast Marv..Sometimes bringing an accused to the stand can be a big mistake

Marlon: I know

Marvin: Of course..Only when the prosecution can poke holes and make the defendant look bad..This is not the case here..Our client was falsely accused..There is absolutely nothing to worry about..All the prosecution had was the  video..The video did not do much damage

Chris: I think we are ready for tomorrow..I think Alex wants to tell his side of the story

Marlon: Definitely

_Meanwhile


Giselle: Kat..Listen baby..We have to run before the guys return..Don't forget..You have to pretend that you are drugged..You hear me?

Katy: Yes

Martine: We are leaving..We will be back tomorrow to check on you

Katy: Thank you

Martine: We told the lady to prepare you something..You have to eat

Giselle: See you tomorrow Kat..Don't worry..I will take care of that doctor

Katy: Bye..Thank you


_The next morning at the courthouse


Bailiff: This court is now in session

Judge: Thank you..Have a seat please..We are making great progress..This morning the defense will call its second witness..Please..Just respect the rules of my courtroom..Having said that..Defense..Are you ready to call your next witness?

Marlon: Yes your honor..The defense would like to call Mr. Alex Smith

Prosecutor: Objection

Judge: Objection to what counselor?

Prosecutor: Your honor the defense did not tell the prosecution that they would call the defendant to the stand

Judge: Please..Both parties..Approach the bench please..Listen up guys..We are not little kids here..Defense..Did you not give a list of your potential witness to the prosecution?

Marvin: We did your honor

Prosecutor: We were not aware that they were about to call the defendant at this time

Marlon: Your honor..The reason why we called our client to the stand at this time..It is simply because we were planning on calling Mrs. Castillo..But..She was not available to take the stand

Judge: This is why the order in which you called your witnesses has changed?

Chris: Yes your honor..And our client will be our last witness

Judge: Both parties are on the same page now?

Prosecutor: Yes your honor

Judge: The prosecution should not have any problem to cross examine the defendant..You brought a case against him..You should have all the questions you wish him to answer..Having said that..The defense may proceed

Chris: Thank you your honor..Your honor..The defense would like to call Mr. Alex Smith to the stand

Bailiff: Please raise your hand and repeat after me


_Minute later


Judge: Have a seat sir

Alex: Thank you

Chris: Good morning..How are you today?

Alex: I am ok..It could have been better..But..I am in jail

Chris: I understand..This is not a nice place to be..This is why the defense team is here..This is why the jury is here..We are here to end your ordeal..Are you ready to answer a few questions for us today?

Alex: Yes sir

Chris: Your name is Alex smith..Right?

Alex: Yes sir

Chris: You mind if I call you Alex

Alex: I don't mind

Chris: Alex..What do you do?..What is your profession?

Alex: I am an accountant sir

Chris: Alex..Prior to now have you ever been in trouble with the law?

Alex: No sir

Chris: Any prior arrests?

Alex: No sir

Chris: Any assault charges?

Alex: No sir

Chris: We may say..You have a clean criminal record prior to that..May we not?

Alex: Yes sir

Chris: Where do you work Alex?

Alex: I work at..Well..I used to work I may say at the Castillo and Burney Accountant Firm

Chris: How long did you work there?

Alex: I worked there for eight months then everything came to a stop

Chris: Your entire world crashed..Did it not?

Alex: Yes

Chris: You expected to work there for a long time..Did you not?

Alex: Yes sir

Chris: You loved your job there..Did you not?

Alex: Yes sir..I enjoyed working there

Chris: Who was you supervisor while you were working there Alex?

Alex: my immediate supervisor was Katy Castillo

Chris: Your honor for the record..Katy Castillo is also the alleged victim..How was your relation with Mrs. Castillo at work?

Alex: It was great..She is a very nice person..She would say that I am her favorite worker

Chris: You had a great professional relation

Alex: Yes sir

Chris: Where was your office located while working there Alex?

Alex: My office was right outside Mrs. Castillo's office..In fact if I leaned to the right just a little bit I could see inside her office

Chris: You worked at that office during your eight month there..Did you?

Alex: No sir..Mrs. Castillo had moved me form there

Chris: From your office to where?

Alex: Inside her office..Her office was pretty big in size..So she wanted me to be in there

Chris: Did you question her decision?

Alex: Not really..She is the boss..After all I was working for her..And it was a good decision..We worked very closely..We had to share data all the time..She was tired of calling me on the phone every minute

Chris: Following you moving into her office..Did anything change regarding your relation with Mrs. Castillo?

Alex: Yes..One day she asked me to work late..We were alone in the office..And one thing led to another we ended up becoming romantically involved

Chris: Something happened between the two of you that day?..Did it not?

Alex: Yes sir

Jim: She is dead

Tony: Stay focused Jim..You want to go to prison..This is why divorce was created

Judge: Order please..Did I hear talking in the gallery?..Please..Respect the rules of my courtroom or you will end in jail..The defense may proceed

Chris: It was consent sex..You did not rape her..In fact she was the one making the moves..Right?

Alex: Yes sir

Chris: No further questions your honor..Your honor..I would like to yield the floor to my colleague Marlon

Judge: Proceed

Marvin: Thank you your honor..Mr. Smith..You indicated that the romantic relationship with Mrs. Castillo started at the office..Did you not?

Alex: Yes sir

Marvin: The relationship had gone beyond the office..Had it not?..Meaning..Did you meet Mrs. Castillo outside of work?

Alex: Yes sir

Marvin: Where else beside work..Have you met with Mrs. Castillo?

Alex: At my friend's house..And at a couple of places

Chris: Did you ever go to Mrs. Castillo's home?

Alex: Yes sir

Chris: When was that?

Alex: Three weeks ago..Her husband had gone on a trip to Europe and she invited me over

Marvin: Your honor..The defense wants to reintroduce the seven minutes video that the prosecution has on record

Judge: Proceed please

Chris: Alex..You recognize who is in that video

Alex: It's me sir

Chris: Can you elaborate for the court where you were and what you were doing at the very time

Alex: Yes sir..We were clowning around and she asked me to remove my shirt to see my abs

Chris: Where were you..I mean in what part of the house you were?

Alex: That was in her closet..She has a huge closet..Almost the same size as the bedroom

Chris: You were not in the process of raping anyone..Or just done raping anyone as the prosecution put it..Were you?

Alex: No sir..I never raped anyone

Chris: You went downstairs that day to get drinks..Did you not?

Alex: Yes sir..I went downstairs to get a couple of drinks..She sent me to get them..Because she was thirsty..And she also told me to get one for myself

Chris: Who was in the kitchen when you went to the kitchen?

Alex: The chef was there..I believe her name is Miss Palmer

Chris: What did you eat that day?

Alex: She ordered the chef to make lamb for me..I told her I never ate lamb..And she wanted me to try it

Chris: How long did you stay at Mrs. Castillo's home?

Alex: I spent three days with her

Chris: What kind of person is Mrs. Castillo?

Alex: She is a very nice human being..She wanted to have some fun..She is a very fun person..She loves her husband very much..She believes that people should be able to have as much fun as they please

Chris: Do you think that Mrs. Castillo would willingly accuse you of rape?

Alex: No sir

Chris: You did not rape Mrs. Castillo..Did you?

Alex: No sir

Chris: You had no reason to rape Miss Castillo..Did you?

Alex: No sir

Chris: You don't believe that Mrs. Castillo would accuse you of rape..Do you?

Alex: No sir

Chris: No further questions your honor

Judge: Thank you sir..At this time the prosecution may cross examine the witness

Prosecutor: Thank you your honor..Mr. Smith..If you raped someone..You would not come here and admit it..Would you sir?

Marvin: Objection

Judge: Sustained

Marvin: The prosecutor's question is not clear your honor..It's started with an "if"..We all know that Mr. Smith did not rape anyone

Judge: The prosecutor may proceed

Prosecutor: Thank you your honor..This is your word against Mrs. Castillo's words..Isn't it Mr. Smith..Or should I say rapist Smith

Chris: Objection your honor

Judge: Sustained

Chris: Your honor the prosecutor is simply trying to contaminate the jury's mind by asking ridiculous questions

Prosecutor: Your honor..There is nothing ridiculous about the question I asked the defendant

Chris: Your honor..The prosecutor also referred to my client as the rapist..My client is innocent until proving guilty you honor

Judge: Prosecutor..You should refrain from referring to the defendant by any derogatory adjectives..Understood?

Prosecutor: Yes your honor

Judge: Proceed

Prosecutor: Mr. Smith..It is Mrs. Castillo's words against yours..Isn't it?

Alex: I guess so

Prosecutor: She said you raped her..Did she not?

Alex: I don't know..I did not see her after my arrest..Why would she say that though?

Prosecutor: Why?..Because you did it

Alex: I did not do anything sir

Prosecutor: She said you did..And you say you did not..You just don't want to go to jail..Do you Mr. Smith?

Alex: What do you mean?..Nobody wants to go to jail..Especially for something you did not do

Prosecutor: Well because you don't want to go to jail..You chose to lie about the crime you've committed..Have you not?

Alex: Sir..I don't know what you are talking about

Prosecutor: The rape Mr. Smith..You suffer with amnesia all of the sudden

Alex: What rape sir?

Marvin: Objection your honor

Judge: Sustained

Marvin: Your honor..The prosecutor has no further questions for the defendant..He is simply harassing him..And he is trying to make our client angry by accusing him of rape repetitively

Judge: Prosecutor..Do you have more questions for the defendant?

Prosecutor: Just one your honor..Mr. Smith..You raped Mrs. Castillo..You just don't want to go to jail..Do you sir

Alex: I don't know what you are talking about

Prosecutor: No further questions your honor


_Meanwhile Dr. Angelo's car is bumped in the back by another vehicle after leaving the Castillo's home..He got out of his car to investigate the damages and he is confronted by two men


Dr. Angelo: You guys are driving like maniacs

Stranger: You really think so

Dr. Angelo: Yes..This is a quiet residential street..There is no reason for you guys to be driving so fast..You guys are idiots

Stranger: Let me introduce you to another idiot..This idiot right here is called Ruger

Dr. Angelo: Be careful with the gun

Stranger: You be careful with it..It is pointing at you..Not at me..Get in the car evil doctor

Dr. Angelo: What is this about?

Stranger: I ask the questions here..Get the car or you will be performing a "Lap Chole" on yourself

Dr. Angelo: Where are you taking me?..Please..I will pay you..Don't hurt me

Stranger: You don't want to get hurt..And you are hurting others

Dr. Angelo: Please..Please

Stranger: Listen Doc..Why do you go to the Castillo's home every day?

Dr. Angelo: To see a patient

Stranger: What patient?..How did she become your patient?..Talk fast or you are going to need a "Total Knee" done

Dr. Angelo: Please..It is a patient who suffered great trauma..Her husband asked me to take care of her

Stranger: You know that patient you are talking about is my sister's best friend..Do you know that?

Dr. Angelo: I did not know that sir

Stranger: You like to drug people uh?..You like that?

Dr. Angelo: No sir..No sir

Stranger: I think you do..Listen carefully..Do you have any of the drugs on you right now

Dr. Angelo: Yes..Yes sir

Stranger: Take off all your clothes

Dr. Angelo: For what?

Stranger: Hurry up or you will have some round burn marks on them

Dr. Angelo: Please don't shoot..All of it?..My underwear too?

Stranger: Yes..Hurry up..Now..Inject yourself with that syringe

Dr. Angelo: Please guys..I am a doctor

Stranger: I love doctors..But..You are an evil one..Hurry up..Are you done?

Dr. Angelo: Yes..Oh my god

Stranger: No..You are not done..One more..Hurry up

Dr. Angelo: Guys..I might get overdosed

Stranger: You prefer to get overdosed on hot lead poisoning..My little idiot called Ruger is here waiting..Hurry up

Dr. Angelo: Ok..Ok..Give me my clothes

Stranger: We are taking those clothes with us..Now..Get out my car

Dr. Angelo: Please..I feel so dizzy

Stranger: Now you know how it feels..Get out

Dr. Angelo: Please give me my clothes

Stranger: See you evil doctor..Buy new clothes with the money you made drugging my sister's friend


_Meanwhile in the courtroom


Judge: Thank you sir..The defense may do a redirect if it chooses to do so

Marlon: The defense will rest your honor

Judge: It is now eleven thirty..The court will adjourn for lunch time..And we will reconvene two o'clock..Please..Ma'am..You know the drill..Remain seated until the jury leaves the room..You don't want to go to jail do you?

Attendant: No your honor..I am in a hurry

Judge: If you don't follow my courtroom's rules..You are only in a hurry to go to jail..Funny uh?..Have a good lunch everyone..See you all at two o'clock..Not two o five..Be punctual

_Two hours later

Judge: Have a seat everyone..We are at the junction to hand the case to the jury for deliberation..Before we do so..Do you have any motions?..If not..We will move to the closing statements

Marlon: Your honor..We don't have a motion..But..Our client mother would like to make a statement on behalf of her son..Also..His friend Frantz Miller wants to say a few words

Judge: Ok..I have no problem with that at all..They don't have to take the stand..They can simply stand behind the microphone stand over there to make the statements..Whenever they are ready..The defense has the floor for family and friend statement

Marlon: Thank you your honor..At this time..Mrs. Smith would like to address the court

Judge: Proceed

Mrs. Smith: Thank you your honor..My name is Julia Smith..I am a psychologist..I have been practicing for twenty two years..I am the mother of two boys..Not so much boys anymore..They are now grown men..They are Alex and my other son Sylvester..Their father passed away when they were only six and eight years old..I raised them by myself..I did remarry..As a single mother I had to worker a little bit harder to provide my two sons with a comfortable life..I raised my sons very well I may say..I taught them to respect others..I taught them to love others..I taught them to be compassionate..Most of all I taught them to respect women..Today is very difficult day for me..Excuse my emotion

Judge: Give her the box of tissues for me please

Mrs. Smith: Thank you..Those tears that are running down my face today are tears of sadness..They are tears of pain..Because I know..My son did not rape anyone..I know..I raised him to know better..He has no reason to rape anyone..He was always the popular nice guy in school..Every girl likes him..Today..I am really hurt to see my son facing prison time for rape..A crime he did not commit..Please ladies and gentlemen of the jury..I am begging you..Please save my son's life..He is innocent..Please..Give him a chance to have a family..A chance to have children one day..He might have been involved in a relationship with a married woman..I am not trying to say it is the right thing to do..But..My son is far from being a rapist..He is a happy guy..Always wants to have fun and cheer others..I know many of you are parents..I know you would understand the pain of having your child in prison for a crime you know he did not commit..I rely on your compassion..I rely on your understanding today..In order for my son to have a tomorrow..A tomorrow where he can once again become a valuable member of society..A tomorrow where he can resume his daily activities and go back to work..Even though I am sadden..But..My heart is filled with hope..Knowing that you can make a difference..You can make a difference by finding him not guilty of rape..I know that he had an improper relationship with a married woman..But..This is not a crime punishable with serving time in prison..Please this is the plea from a mother to you..Help me save my son's life..Thank you

Judge: Thank you ma'am..Right now..The defendant's friend may have the floor

Frantz: Thank your honor..Good afternoon ladies and gentlemen..My name is Frantz Miller..I have known Alex Smith for sixteen years now..He is my best friend..He is my brother..Even if he is found guilty..He will still be my brother..I know Alex better than most people..We grow up together..He is one guy who is always against bullying of women..He is the guy who got into many fights because he was protecting girls from being bullied..To see him sitting in a courtroom..Accused of rape..It is simple absurd..Today is very sad day for me..A sad day for all his friends..Many of whom are present in the courtroom..As you may see..Many of them have tears in their eyes..I am sorry..Excuse my emotion please..I don't shed tears often..Today..I can't stop those tears from running down my face..They are tears of anger..And also tears of sadness..I am angry because I know my friend did not rape Mrs. Castillo..Mrs. Castillo and my friend Alex were friends..She came to my place on more than one occasion to meet my friend..He had no reason to rape her..This is simply an accusation created by Mrs. Castillo's husband..My friend is not a rapist and will never be one..He loves the ladies..This is a fact that I cannot deny..But..To say..To accuse him of being a rapist is a stretch beyond this world we are living in..Therefore ladies and gentlemen of the jury..I am asking you to use your judgment to find my friend Alex Smith not guilty on all count..Thank you

Judge: Thank you sir..At this time the court will adjourn for the day..We will reconvene tomorrow morning..Both parties will do their closing statements and the case will be handed to the jury for deliberation..I thank you Mrs. Smith and Mr. Miller for their statement on behalf of the defendant

Marlon: Your honor..Our client wants to know if it is ok for him to say a few words

Judge: Yes he may..Sir..It is ok to say a few words..But..I don't want you to incriminate yourself..I hope your attorneys have advised you regarding that aspect

Alex: Yes your honor..They have

Judge: Proceed please

Alex: Thank you your honor..I just want to take this opportunity to tell my mom and all my friends who are here today..That I did not rape anyone..I want to apologize to my mom for the pain that I have caused her..Mom I am sorry..I should not have been involved romantically with a married woman..But..I did not..I repeat I did not rape anyone..To my buddy Frantz..I am sorry brother..You were totally against that relationship..If I am found guilty and I have to go to prison for many years..I want you to remember this..I did not rape anyone..I want you to keep your head up..I did not rape anyone..And dad..I know you are somewhere watching..I did not rape anyone..Please help me dad..Help your son..Thank you

Judge:  Thank you..Order please..I understand some of you got emotional..And are crying..Please..This is not a funeral..This is a courtroom..Order..As I have stated prior to the defendant's statement..The court will now adjourn..It will reconvene tomorrow morning at nine o'clock..At that time the defense and the prosecution will do their closing statements..Before I put an end to this session..Does anyone have anything to say..Anymore statements from family members and friends?..I guess the silence means no..Thank you everyone..Remain seated until the jury leaves the room..Have a good evening


_Outside the courtroom


Mrs. Smith:  Thank you guys

Marlon:  You are welcome Mrs. Smith

Mrs. Smith:  How do we look?

Marlon:  Regarding the verdict? We are looking very good..But..Verdicts can also be surprising..We will keep on praying and keep our fingers crossed..And hope the jury sees through what is happening

Mrs. Smith:  Thank you so much guys

Marvin:  You are very welcome

Chris:  Mrs. Smith..We are going to get something to eat..Would you like to come with us?

Mrs. Smith:  No thank you..Those few days I barely eat at all..I don't have appetite..I can't sleep at night since my son arrest

Marvin:  We are here for you..We will make sure that he goes home

Mrs. Smith:  Thank you


_Meanwhile


Jim:  Hello

Tony: Hey Jim

Jim: Tony..What's going on?

Tony: You heard what happened to Angelo?

Jim: Angelo?..Who is Angelo?..I don't know any Angelo

Tony: The doctor

Jim: Dr. Angelo?..What happened to him?

Tony: Some guys slapped him a couple times

Jim: Really?..This does not have anything to do with us

Tony: Yes..He got slapped for drugging Katy

Jim: Really?..Who could be behind this?

Tony: I have no idea

Jim: It's ok..The trial is over..We don't need him anymore..Katy will not be able to testify..It's too late now

Tony: You are right


_The next morning at the courthouse


Judge: Good morning everyone..Today..We will move forward toward putting an end to this trial..This is the day of the closing statements..I hope both parties are ready..Prosecution..Are you ready for your closing statement?

Prosecutor: Yes your honor

Judge: Order please..Who is talking in my courtroom?..Ma'am..That's you..You were talking while I was talking

Attendee: I am sorry sir

Judge: Leave please..Hurry up..Prosecutor you have the floor

Prosecutor: Thank you your honor..Good morning ladies and gentlemen..Good morning ladies and gentlemen of the jury..Today is very exciting day for the prosecution..This is the day that we've been waiting for..This is the day where the defendant..Mr. Smith will pay the price for the crime he has committed against Mrs. Castillo..She could not be here in the courtroom..Therefore ladies and gentlemen of the jury..Be a voice to Mrs. Castillo..A voice that will send a clear and loud message to the defendant..That crime like this will not be tolerated in our community..The defendant did not just rape the victim..But he did it at her house..He even went to the Castillo's fridge to get drinks after raping her..Today..You the members of this jury have a very important duty..That is to make sure animal such Mr. Smith does not walk our streets..We owe this to the victim..We owe this to all the women in our community..You've seen the evidence..You've watched the videos..Therefore..You must do what is necessary..You must send Mr. Smith to prison for a long time so he could think about that horrendous act he has committed..You must keep in mind..That the victim will never shake off that traumatic event..Don't be fooled by the defense rhetoric..The defense is insinuating the defendant is innocent..Don't fall for it..They just don't want their client to go to jail..When we hand the case to you today..The prosecution will rest assured that justice will be done..The only way for justice to be done is to find the defendant guilty of first degree rape..I am not going to talk much longer..This is not about talking today..It's all about actions..It's all about finding justice for the victim..It's all about finding justice to Mrs. Castillo..It's all about sending a message to the defendant..The prosecution rely on you the good people of this jury to find the defendant guilty and send him where he belongs..Behind bars..Thank you


Judge:  Thank you sir..The defense has the floor

Marvin:  Thank you your honor..Good morning ladies and gentlemen..Just like the prosecutor..Today we excited as well..The defense team is excited for a much different reason..We are excited because we have been waiting patiently for justice to knock..And justice is finally at the door..The prosecutor is here..Let me remind you ladies and gentlemen..For one reason and one reason only..That is to send someone to prison..Guilty or not..This is not why we are here..We are here to find justice..We are here to prevent the destruction of the life of yet another young man..We are here for a good cause..And together we will achieve what we came here to do..Too many times we have stood aside and let the inferno of injustice swallow our young people..Today is a new day..This is the day when we are saying no to such atrocity..This is the day where we say enough is enough..Sometimes..When the pain is not ours we tend to not care..We must change that way of thinking..We must stand together to stop this malfeasance..We must fill that pit-hole up and prevent it from swallowing our young men..I understand that the prosecutor would love to send Mr. Smith to prison just to have a topic to talk about around the water fountain at the office..Today is not that day..This is the year two thousand sixteen..And there is no time for false accusation simple to ruin one's life..Now is the time where we are going to stand together and put a stop to that practice..You've been in the courtroom through the whole trial..You've listened to the prosecution's case against our client..You must find the defendant guilty beyond all reasonable doubts..And the prosecution left us with so much doubt..We would love to please the prosecutor..But..We cannot afford to lose one more young man..We would love to participate in that ballade toward injustice..But..Our heart will not allow it..Our sense of duty will not allow it..We understand clearly that our client and Mrs. Castillo were friends..They were involved in a romantic relationship..That's about it..They were two people having fun..I am not saying it was morally right..Because..Mrs. Castillo is a married lady..But that does not warrant prison time to our client..It is not punishable with prison time for having a romantic relationship with a married woman..I understand that is what some people would like to see happen..But..We are still in America..And it is not a crime in America to have a romantic relationship with a married woman..Therefore..Our client should at all be sitting on that sit as a defendant..He should not at all be in a courtroom..Somewhere down the line..There was a dirty and powerful hand that put him there..But..We are not shaken..Or afraid..We are not afraid because we are in the right place..Not only in the right place..But..We are in front of twelve people whom will make sure justice is served..As we hand the case to you today..We will leave with the faith that justice will be served..We will leave with our heart flooded with the hope that justice will be triumphant..We will leave here knowing that our client will be a free man once again..Finding Mr. Smith not guilty is the only right thing to do..We cannot afford to do otherwise..We cannot afford to travel back into those dark days where injustice was a current practice..Today is a new day..And now is the time to say no to injustice..Now is the time to prevent the powerful jaw of injustice from closing around that young man..Now is the time to dry the tears off his mother's eyes..Now is the time to bring solace to his friends..Now is the time if you allow me..To restore his life by finding him not guilty of rape..This is the faith with which we are leaving here today..We will rest assured and know that the good people of the jury will rise to that task ahead of them..And find Mr. Smith not guilty..Thank you your honor

Judge: Thank you counselor..Well done..At this time..The case will be handed to the jury for deliberation..The court will adjourn for jury deliberation..Please..Don't go too far..Just in case we reach a verdict

_The jury deliberated through the whole afternoon..And the next morning a verdict was reached

-Guys..My loving readers..This is the day of the verdict..We cannot miss it..We have to be inside the courtroom for that one..Follow me

Bailiff: All rise..This court is now in session

Judge: Thank you..Good morning everyone..Both parties are present?

Prosecutor: Yes your honor

Marlon: Yes your honor

Judge: I understand that the jury has reached a verdict..Who is the foreman

Jury Foreman: Me your honor

Judge: May I have a copy of the verdict please

Jury Foreman: Yes you may your honor

Judge: Thank you..Foreman..Proceed with the verdict..Please..Following the reading of the verdict..I don't want any cheering..Maintain the order please..Mr. Smith..Please rise..Foreman..Proceed please

Jury Foreman: We the jury finds the defendant Alex Smith..Guilty of first degree rape


_Following those words..Alex's mother collapsed..Everyone in the court was shocked..Alex's friends were in disbelief..They had tears in their eyes..Alex had his head buried in his hands..His lawyers were speechless..They did not understand what just happened..The court officers and the sheriffs slowly approached the defense table and handcuffed Alex..He turned around towards his friends and said sorry guys..Everyone in the courtroom was crying..As the officers were taking Alex out of the courtroom a loud female voice filled the courtroom..Its Katy..Let's listen:


Katy: HOLD ON..HOLD PLEASE..HOLD ON

Judge: Order please

Katy: I have something to say

Court Officer: Ma'am..Come with me

Katy: He is innocent

Judge: Let go of her..Let her talk

Jim: Katy..What are you doing here?..Go home now

Katy: No..No..He is innocent..I can't let this happen..He is innocent..He did not rape me

Jim: Leave now I said

Judge: Sir..Be quiet or you will be held in contempt..I am the wrong woman to mess with

Katy: Your honor..He is innocent..I can't let an innocent person go to prison for such a long time for something he did not do

Judge: Order please..Order..What do you mean?..Who are you?

Katy: My name is Katy Castillo..The alleged victim..I was never raped by Alex..They made up the story..I can't let that happen..I love him..He did not rape me your honor

Judge: Please..Controlled your emotion..Once again..This is not a funeral..Control your crying..I don't want to hear noise of people crying in my courtroom

Jim: I SAID..GO HOME NOW KATY

Judge: Officer..Take him inside for me..He will be held in contempt

Marlon: Your honor..The defense wants to make a motion for mistrial

Judge: No need for motion counselor..Mistrial it is..Officers..Remove the handcuffs from Mr. Smith's arms..The DA needs to get to the bottom of this..This is outrageous..No need for motion..This is a mistrial

Marlon: Thank you your honor

Frantz: Alex..What are you doing man?..You are not going?

Alex: What time is it?..I fell asleep

Frantz: I know..You love my couch

Alex: Dude..You would not believe that..I had such a dream..I dreamed that my boss and I had a love affair

Frantz: You mean with Jim Castillo's wife?

Alex: Yes

Frantz: Man..That must be a crazy dream

Alex: In the dream..Jim Castillo found out that I was with his wife..I was accused of rape and found guilty

Frantz: Well..You are lucky you did not die in the dream

Alex: It was a crazy dream..I was found guilty..She came to the courtroom and said that I was innocent..She said that she is in love with me

Frantz: Really?..I would love to hear what happened after..Because I know Jim Castillo will try to kill you

Alex: Part two of that dream is coming soon

Frantz: I can't wait..Let's go brother.


It was a pleasure to share those words with you..I look forward to have you with me again into yet another wonderful adventure

Thank You!!

Phito Polycarpe

www.ingramcontent.com/pod-product-compliance
Lightning Source LLC
Chambersburg PA
CBHW071324310526
45789CB00016B/610